"Saint Paul will never have a better apologist than Canon Robertson nor will there ever be a more insightful and thorough application of a Paulinian apologia to the practical work of the contemporary church than this one. One may not agree with all the lines and conclusions of Chuck Robertson's argument, but no one can unsay his thoroughness, the ease and depth of his scholarship, or the sincerity and usefulness of its presentation here. This is an ideal volume for private reading as well as for group study."

—Phyllis Tickle, author of *The Great Emergence: How Christianity Is Changing and Why*

"Popular perceptions of Barnabas and Paul are often misleading and prejudicial. In his readable and absorbing book, Robertson has restored the truth about these two Christian workers who—in their distinctly separate ways—cleared the way for the growth of the church and the advance of the gospel around the world."

—Jim Winkler, President and General Secretary of the National Council of Churches, USA

Other Books in This Series

Calvin vs Wesley by Don Thorsen

Barnabas

vs.

Paul

To Encourage
or Confront?

C. K. Robertson

Foreword by Desmond Tutu

Abingdon Press
Nashville

BARNABAS VS. PAUL:
TO ENCOURAGE OR CONFRONT?

Copyright © 2015 by Abingdon Press

This book is printed on acid-free paper.

Library of Congress Cataloging-in-Publication Data

Robertson, C. K. (Charles Kevin), 1964-
  Barnabas vs. Paul : to encourage or confront? / C.K. Robertson ; foreword by Desmond Tutu.—First
[edition].
    pages cm
  Includes bibliographical references.
  ISBN 978-1-63088-277-8 (binding: soft back/ trade pbk. : alk. paper) 1. Bible. Epistles of Paul—
Criticism, interpretation, etc. 2. Bible. Acts—Criticism, interpretation, etc. 3. Paul, the Apostle, Saint.
4. Barnabas, Apostle, Saint. I. Title.
  BS2650.52.R63 2015
  225.9'22—dc23

                                                                                        2014035378

15 16 17 18 19 20 21 22 23 24—10 9 8 7 6 5 4 3 2 1
MANUFACTURED IN THE UNITED STATES OF AMERICA

To +Kirk Smith and +Katharine Jefferts Schori,

more than just bishops to me . . . encouragers

Contents

Foreword

How we read the Bible is important! As I have said elsewhere, we must use the Bible to help us interpret the Bible and not simply take Bible texts in isolation and out of context to fit with our particular biases. This is what the Reverend Canon Chuck Robertson calls us to do in regards to our interpretation of Saint Paul. He is correct when he says in his introduction that what people think they know about the apostle is often not accurate, as they take a verse here and a verse there out of context and then dare to draw conclusions about Paul. There have always been people who have misused the Bible to support their own injustices and prejudices, and there have been some who have particularly used Paul to push others down and keep them down.

I have seen firsthand the evils of oppression, of saying that some people are inferior to other people. I have always believed that we should be committed to the total liberation of God's children, and it is precisely Saint Paul who calls us to enjoy that glorious liberty. When he and Barnabas spoke to a large group of pagans in Lystra, he did not condemn them because they were different from him; no, Paul called them God's offspring. He offered the open hand of welcome, not a clenched fist of self-righteousness. In more than one instance, Paul professed that God created us all for fellowship and togetherness, not for separation and discrimination.

Through a careful and accessible reading of the Acts of the Apostles and Paul's own letters, Canon Robertson helps us see Saint Paul as he was, a liberator who understood that the gospel brings those who are far-off and those who are near closer to one another. In an earlier book, Robertson described

ix

Paul as a "dangerous" person, and he is right! May we all be dangerous saints for God, pushing unapologetically against any forms of injustice that we encounter. And I am especially grateful that we can see Paul in light of his friendship and partnership with Barnabas, the Great Encourager. The two biblical characters come alive and remind us that they were flesh and blood people like us, trying to follow God and make a difference in their world even as we try to do so in our world today.

We cannot ever afford to sit back and let someone else misuse the Bible for their own purposes. We must ever "read, mark, learn, and inwardly digest" Holy Scripture. This glimpse into the lives and ministries of Paul and Barnabas can help us do that, as we learn from them and stand for the glorious liberation to which God calls us all.

God bless you,
DESMOND
Most Rev. Desmond Tutu
Archbishop Emeritus of Cape Town and Nobel Peace Laureate

A Word about Acts

I nasmuch as the book of Acts is an integral part of all that follows, I should be clear up front about some basic assumptions that I bring to this book.

First, I am a Christian, and more specifically an Episcopalian, and for me Acts is part of the Christian canon of scripture, the inspired word of God, examined and interpreted through the lenses of tradition and reason. As such, I approach Acts carefully, prayerfully, always beginning any reading of it with a word of prayer, such as Proper 28 from *The Book of Common Prayer*: "Blessed Lord, who caused all holy Scriptures to be written for our learning: Grant us so to hear them, read, mark, learn, and inwardly digest them, that we may embrace and ever hold fast the blessed hope of everlasting life, which you have given us in our Savior Jesus Christ; who lives and reigns with you and the Holy Spirit, one God, for ever and ever. *Amen.*"[1]

Second, as that prayer suggests, I approach Acts not as cotton candy to be swallowed with ease, but as spiritual meat or vegetables to be chewed on with deliberation, in order to "inwardly digest" the wisdom therein. Acts is worth our time and our honest study, as we dare to wrestle with things we might find difficult at first glance.

Third, it is important to say that, while grounded in my own years of research into Acts, as well as Paul's letters, this book is not intended to be an academic treatise. Rather, I hope you find it to be interesting, accessible, and practical in your own personal or small-group study. This is not a book heavy with endnotes, though biblical references and some outside resources are offered for any further study that you may wish to do.

Fourth, I believe it is important to recognize Acts as the second part of an ongoing *success story* of the early church attributed to the evangelist Luke. Following his "orderly account" in the Gospel (Luke 1:1) of Jesus's life, death, and resurrection, the evangelist Luke then picks up where that story ends, and begins a lively tale with fascinating characters and, eventually, one clear protagonist. Although it is called the Acts of the Apostles, from about halfway on it could more accurately be called the Acts of Paul, as it becomes something of a defense of the apostle's life and ministry.

Fifth, Acts is not, strictly speaking, history in the modern sense, although it is finally being recognized that there truly is no such thing as completely objective reporting. Even the best news accounts or histories are in some way subjective, if only in terms of what is selected to report or not report. The goal here is not somehow to go through Acts to learn about "the historical Paul" but rather to take seriously the Paul of Acts on his own terms, even as we study Paul's own letters, which immediately follow Acts in the New Testament.

Sixth, though much of Acts is indeed focused on Paul, there are many other fascinating characters who make their way on and off stage, including our other protagonist, Joseph the Levite of Cyprus, more commonly known as Barnabas. Acts is silent about his years before he joined the church and about his years after he and Paul split up and went their separate ways. But, clearly given the book you hold in your hands, I think he is someone well worth getting to know—and from what you will see of him in Acts, Luke apparently thought so as well!

Introduction

Setting the Stage

While driving past a church one day, I noticed the invitation on the marquee out front: "Welcome! Please come in—just leave your assumptions at the door." The same could be said at the start of a book about two such intriguing characters. They were inseparable, until they went their separate ways. They were close friends and colleagues, until a conflict tore them apart. Barnabas of Cyprus faded into relative obscurity, while Paul of Tarsus became, apart from Jesus himself, the most influential and well-known figure in the history of Christianity.

And therein lies the problem.

Peter, Paul, and Mary

What people *think* they know about Paul is not necessarily accurate. In fact, in many cases it is downright wrong. But the negative views persist. Years ago, someone once said to me, "I would love to have heard Paul preach, but afterwards I would have given him a piece of my mind about his view on women!" What this person was referring to, of course, is the commonly held stereotype of Paul as a misogynist, just one in a long list of negative labels heaped on him through the years. Of course, much of this is understandable. After all, a quick glance at passages such as, "Women should be quiet during the meeting. They are not allowed to talk,"[1] or "slaves, obey your masters,"[2] is enough to lead modern Christians to shake their heads and put as much distance as they can between themselves and the apostle, like an obnoxious uncle who family members are embarrassed to admit is related to them. Everyone

1

has a soft spot in their heart for Simon Peter, that impetuous, headstrong fisherman who followed Jesus, then denied Jesus, then led the early movement in Jesus's name. His contemporary, Paul, on the other hand, became the scapegoat upon whom believers and onlookers alike have put the blame for just about anything wrong with the faith.

But, again, let me say that these persons would be wrong. For as we will see, contrary to popular opinion, this spiritual pioneer was more liberator than enslaver, more egalitarian than xenophobe. Although he started out as a strong supporter of the social and religious conventions that defined and divided people, he soon became a bold overthrower of the same! If we are willing to spend some time with Paul, if we are willing to leave our assumptions at the door and engage in a more careful examination, we might be surprised to find him quite different from the caricature that has since been drawn of him.

In this sense, Paul is much like Mary Magdalene. Ask the vast majority of people what they know of Mary, and they will instantly reply that she was a prostitute. And yet, contrary to what people *think* is clear in the scriptural texts, nowhere in the Gospels is this actually stated. In fact, every mention of her except one occurs during Jesus's crucifixion and resurrection, when Magdalene steps into a prominent position. The exception, the one time she is mentioned prior to the events of the passion, is in Luke 7:51. There she is described as a woman whom Jesus cleansed of "seven demons," and who with a group of other women went on to support his ministry "out of their resources."[3] Now, whatever is meant by the "seven demons," there is no indication that it refers to prostitution. In fact, one early tradition affirms that it was because of her purity that Mary was beset by the Enemy's demons! Yet this passage eventually was conflated with the one preceding it in Luke 7:36-50, which speaks of an unnamed "sinner"—a clear euphemism for a woman of ill repute—who anoints Jesus's feet and washes them with her tears. This image of a penitent prostitute, instead of that of a woman of means who financially supported Jesus's ministry, eventually won out as the image everyone would have of Mary Magdalene. But this did not happen until a few centuries later! Before that, she was respected and even revered. Saint Augustine, the great bishop and theologian, described her as the "apostle to the apostles." Apocryphal gospels and acts were written about her, in which she was depicted as a courageous leader at times surpassing even Peter and the apostles. But to some men in leadership, who only saw her as a woman with a highly visible role in the beginnings of Christianity, saw her as a great threat. Perhaps for that very reason Mary Magdalene was retroactively painted as a prostitute . . . a saint, yes, but one somehow a bit tainted.[4]

Similarly, what if Paul was such a challenge to the status quo that his reputation was "edited" by those who feared where some of his ideas and initiatives might lead? What if the figure who became forever labeled as a misogynist was actually the very person who offered the possibility of complete gender equality within the church? I still recall when I first learned that Paul of the 1960s folk group "Peter, Paul, and Mary" was not actually named Paul at all. His real name was Noel Stookey. But their manager believed that "Peter, Noel, and Mary" lacked something, and therefore for the good of the group Noel was renamed Paul. Now, most people who know anything about early Christianity are aware that Paul of Tarsus was first known by his Hebrew name Saul in his earliest appearances in the Acts of the Apostles. But this change of name is nothing compared to the change in how Saul/Paul would eventually become known. Indeed, the caricature of the Apostle Paul that has been promulgated through the centuries is quite different from the apprentice whom Barnabas took under his wing, and very much in contradiction to Barnabas's bridge-building, boundary-breaking ministry.

Now, there is that other name again. While most people know the names of Peter and Paul, far fewer are familiar with Joseph the Levite, whom the apostles called Barnabas. But it is important to note that Barnabas is hardly an anonymous figure in the book of Acts. Indeed, here in the second volume of Luke's two-part account,[5] Barnabas is mentioned by name more often than most of the "official" apostles. Only Peter and Paul get more time onstage in Acts. In many ways, Barnabas is the bridge that takes us from Peter to Paul, from the shadow of the temple to the ends of the earth. Barnabas is there in Jerusalem in the earliest days of the movement, and later he is in Antioch where the movement turns a corner and is transformed from a small Jewish sect into something altogether new. It is no exaggeration to assert that without Barnabas, there most likely would be no Christianity as we know it.

3

This book, then, is about these two leaders, one well worth getting to know, and the other worth getting to know more accurately. But before we do, it is important to explore the environment in which they emerged. So, let us leave Barnabas and Paul for a moment, and make our way back to Luke's Gospel and the one who started it all.

The Model for Apostleship

Many are those through the years who have spoken of the purity and simplicity of the early Jesus movement, when "all the believers were united and shared everything,"[6] whose members were "one in heart and mind" and "there were no needy persons among them."[7] Peter along with James and John and the other official apostles were the undisputed leaders of the movement, which was known quite simply as "the Way." To many today, the carpenter from Nazareth had no intention of founding a new religion, but simply wanted to share a message of love and peace, and this is what the apostolic community in Jerusalem was all about. Then, the argument goes, Paul came along and messed up everything—adding the doctrine and dogma, the institutionalization and legalism, and all the elements that people today find offensive about Christianity. If only we could somehow get rid of all of Paul's religious accouterments and get back to Jesus and the early Jesus movement, these proponents cry out, then all would be well.[8]

It is an argument that, in the end, makes little sense, for it is based on the notion of a golden age now lost, an idyllic time where all was well, a Camelot, a garden of Eden. Though it is an almost universal myth, religious systems seem particularly susceptible to it. We love to look back with a sense of nostalgia. Ministers new to a congregation undoubtedly hear story after story of the "good old days." But as I have shared elsewhere, a wise lay leader who had been active in his congregation for decades, once admitted, "If there was a golden age in this parish, I must have blinked and missed it."[9] That's right! As in filmmaker Woody Allen's acclaimed 2011 movie, *Midnight in Paris*, even if we could be magically transported to whatever time we believe to have been the "good old days," we would quickly learn that it was far from perfect. Just consider the 1950s, often lifted up as the golden age of American religiosity, and yet as Dr. Martin Luther King Jr. once famously said, "Eleven o'clock on

4

Sunday morning [is] . . . the most segregated hour of America."[10] The garden of Eden is not necessarily idyllic to those on the outside looking in.

We should not be surprised, then, to go back to the story of Jesus and the apostles and find things more complicated than we originally assumed. Luke's Gospel, the predecessor to his second volume, Acts, sets the stage for the conflicts yet to come. In the Gospel's fourth chapter, we see Jesus making his inaugural appearance as a prophet in his hometown synagogue, reading a passage from the writings of Isaiah: "The Spirit of the Lord is upon me, / because the Lord has anointed me. / He has sent me to preach good news to the poor, / to proclaim release to the prisoners / and recovery of sight to the blind, / to liberate the oppressed, / and to proclaim the year of the Lord's favor."[11] In the following verse, Luke reports Jesus's bold assertion: "Today, this scripture has been fulfilled just as you heard it." Such words were met with bemusement and bewilderment, as his listeners remarked, "This is Joseph's son, isn't it?" The mood, however, soon turned ugly with Jesus's next words:

> I assure you that no prophet is welcome in the prophet's hometown. And I can assure you that there were many widows in Israel during Elijah's time, when it didn't rain for three and a half years and there was a great food shortage in the land. Yet Elijah was sent to none of them but only to a widow in the city of Zarephath in the region of Sidon. There were also many persons with skin diseases in Israel during the time of the prophet Elisha, but none of them were cleansed. Instead, Naaman the Syrian was cleansed.[12]

These were provocative, even perilous, words. For here Jesus reminded a crowd proud of its heritage as God's chosen people of two key scriptural instances of God's apparent preference for outsiders, for those whom Jesus's audience would consider children of a lesser god. It does not help that what he said was accurate—his listeners had only to look at the scriptures to see for themselves—but there was nothing then, or now, reasonable about a mob's rage. And this crowd was indeed filled with rage, so much so that Jesus's first public appearance almost became his last, as they attempted to stone him to death, only to have a nonanxious Jesus walk out through their midst. And he did not stop there.

It is often said that, of the four canonical Gospels, Luke's is the one that focuses on Jesus's acceptance of outsiders. Consider, for example, that Luke alone records the parable of the Good Samaritan, an oxymoron to most first-century Jews; after all, there was no such thing as a "good" Samaritan, right? In Luke's Gospel, women, servants, Samaritans, Gentiles—all those considered to be on the lower rungs of the social ladder from the standpoint of a faithful child of Israel—were welcomed and affirmed by Jesus. In fact, Jesus's inclusive spirit was prophesized back in chapter 2 of Luke's Gospel, when the infant Jesus was presented at the temple and a man named Simeon declared the child to be "a light for revelation to the Gentiles / and a the glory for your people Israel."[13] So it is not terribly surprising that two chapters later in Luke's Gospel we find the adult Jesus speaking about God's mercy to those outside the accepted religious and social boundaries. This is precisely what many around him did not want to hear, including his chosen apostles. And this is where things get very interesting.

"Sent Ones"

While the Twelve are first mentioned in Luke 6:13, demarcated there from the larger, unnumbered pool of Jesus's followers,[14] it is three chapters later that Luke spells out what these dozen "apostles"—literally "sent ones" from the Greek—are actually sent to do: "Jesus called the Twelve together and he gave them power and authority over all demons and to heal sicknesses. He sent them out to proclaim God's kingdom and to heal the sick."[15] Proclamation, complemented by deeds of power in the form of healings and exorcisms, is the Twelve's appointed task. It is important to note that the threefold apostolic task of preaching, healing, and exorcism reflects Jesus's own ministry back in Luke 4 as one "sent" with the purpose of proclaiming the reign of God.

Following the selection of the Twelve in Luke 6, Luke emphasizes that Jesus is both accompanied and observed by them: "the Twelve were with him."[16] They enjoy a unique position vis-à-vis Jesus, clearly differentiated from "a great company of his disciples and a huge crowd of people"—while the latter come to Jesus to hear him, to be healed of their diseases, and to have demons cast out of them, the Twelve are actually "with him" as Jesus teaches, heals, and exorcises.[17] They then are commissioned to do the very things he himself had been sent to do.[18] Interestingly, what is missing in Luke's commissioning account is the prohibition found in Matthew's Gospel against going to the Gentiles or even amongst the Samaritans.[19] Rather, between their selection in Luke 6 and their commissioning in Luke 9, the apostles bear witness to Jesus reaching out beyond expected boundaries to outsiders: healing a Roman centurion's servant, being anointing by a prostitute, exorcising a demon in the land of the Gerasenes.

With all this before them, it would make sense that the Twelve would follow in the footsteps of their apostolic model. But this is where things become a bit ambiguous. To understand what comes next in Luke's account, it is important to compare the events of the commissioning and the events following it in Luke 9 with corresponding passages in Mark's and Matthew's Gospels. A simple chart may help illustrate:

	Luke	Mark	Matthew
The commissioning of the Twelve	9:1-6	6:1-13	
Herod's confusion about Jesus and the death of John the Baptist	9:7-9	6:14-16	14:1-2
Herod's part in John's death		6:17-29	14:3-12
The return of the Twelve	9:10	6:30-32	
The feeding of the five thousand	9:11-17	6:33-34	14:13-21
Jesus walking on water		6:45-5	14:22-33
Healings at Gennesaret		6:53-55	14:34-36
Warnings concerning the elder		7:1-23	15:1-20
Jesus and the Syrophoenician woman		7:24-30	15:21-28
Healing of a deaf man		7:31-37	
The feeding of the four thousand		8:1-10	15:32-39
Two-stage healing of a blind man		8:22-26	
Peter's declaration about Jesus	9:18-21	8:27-30	16:13-20
Jesus's passion prediction	9:22-27	8:31–9:1	16:21-28
The transfiguration	9:28-36	9:2-10	17:1-9
The demon-possessed boy and apostles' failure to exorcise	9:37-43	9:14-29	17:14-21
Second passion prediction	9:43b-45	9:30-32	17:22
Argument about greatness	9:46-48	9:33-37	18:1-5
Apostles' concern about an exorcist outside their group	9:49-50	9:38-41	
Samaritan opposition	9:51-55		
Would-be followers	9:57-62		8:19-22
The coming of the Seventy	10:1-12		

The first thing to note is the congruence between Luke's and Mark's order of events. As in Mark's commissioning scene, Jesus's words to the Twelve in Luke are brief as he sends them out: Take little as you go, stay in one house, and wipe the dust off your feet of any town that does not accept you.[20] Not only is the prohibition concerning Gentiles and Samaritans in Matthew's Gospel missing in Luke, but also the warnings about expulsion from the synagogues and division within families for followers of Jesus.[21] For the remainder of Luke 9, all the way until verse 50, the order of events follows that of Mark's Gospel, albeit with several missing elements. Luke does not include, for instance, Mark's detailed interlude concerning Herod's part in the Baptist's death, and also leaves out all the events described by Mark (and passed on by Matthew) between the feeding of the five thousand and Peter's declaration of Jesus as Messiah. When these elements from Mark's account are excised—not to mention the additional sets of teaching found in Matthew—then what is left in Luke 9 is a consistent focus on a single relational system, the Twelve.

And what does Luke reveal about the Twelve? Again and again, he shows us their deficiencies and failures following their commissioning. While in Matthew's Gospel, the Twelve understand what Jesus tells them, in Luke's account "its meaning was hidden from them."[22] As in Mark, the Twelve argue amongst themselves about who is greatest and are threatened by the work of an outside exorcist who, Luke asserts, was simply accomplishing the very thing that they themselves had failed to do only nine verses earlier. In Mark's account, following Jesus's assertion to the Twelve that "whoever isn't against us is for us," there is a word of comfort and reward to "you [who] belong to Christ."[23] No such affirmation is found in Luke's account. Rather, there follows a story unique to Luke concerning the refusal of a Samaritan village to receive Jesus "because he was determined to go to Jerusalem."[24] The apostolic response offered by James and John, to ask whether fire from heaven should be called down upon this village, meets with an immediate rebuke from Jesus. So what is so important about all this, and what does this have to do with Barnabas and Paul? The answer lies in what happens next in Luke 10.

8

Seventy Others

Only Luke includes the tale of a second commissioning of a numbered group by Jesus, immediately following the reporting of the failed mission of Jesus and the Twelve in Samaria. This time, it is not another twelve but rather "seventy others" who are "sent out," even as the Twelve had been sent just one chapter earlier.[25] This passage, unique to Luke, is not a small thing, for while Luke reports mixed results for the Twelve in the chapter sandwiched between the two groups' commissionings, the Seventy receive unqualified praise for their work. While the Twelve were given authority over demons and yet failed to exercise this authority in the case of a possessed boy, the Seventy are reported to enjoy great success over demons. Jesus's exclamation, "I saw Satan fall from heaven like lightning" is not only unique to Luke, but is reserved for the Seventy's joyful return, in contrast to the quiet reception given to the returning Twelve.[26]

What, then, is the significance of the Seventy, and why does Luke make a point of bringing them onstage? First, there is the issue of the numerical symbolism. Twelve is, of course, the number of the tribes of Israel, and in creating a core group of twelve apostles, Jesus seems to be fulfilling the promise of Israel's restoration. He is, after all, often called the Son of David in the Gospels, the successor to the great king. Matthew's Gospel embraces this noble heritage for the apostles, as has been noted already in Jesus's prohibition in his apostolic commission against going to Gentiles or even Samaritans. The Twelve should instead reach out "to the lost sheep, the people of Israel."[27] Seventy (or seventy-two, is it is found in some early texts) also has scriptural precedents, the most obvious being a story in the book of Numbers in which Moses admits the overwhelming nature of his task of leadership, and the result is that God's Spirit rests on seventy elders who then are empowered to prophesy and proclaim.[28] A corollary is that two others, Eldad and Medad, who did not go out with the seventy are nevertheless blessed with the same gift and continue to prophesy even when the others are finished with the task. Joshua, Moses's young apprentice, complains and says they should be ordered to cease and desist, only to have Moses rebuke him, "If only all the Lord's people were prophets!"[29] The parallel to the tale in Luke 9 in which James and John complain about someone outside the Twelve casting out demons, only to be rebuked by Jesus, is clear.

9

But there is another, equally intriguing precedent for the Seventy. The tenth chapter of Genesis lists the nations of the world following the flood, numbered respectively as seventy in the Hebrew text and seventy-two in the Greek translation known as the Septuagint.[30] Jesus's proclamation in his commissioning of the Seventy that "the harvest is bigger than you can imagine, but there are few workers" acknowledges that more "sent ones" are needed, that the Twelve, like Moses, simply cannot do all that needs to be done. And the fact that this is not another group of twelve, but Seventy, further suggests that the mission field truly is larger than simply the lost sheep of Israel.[31]

Second, the result of the Seventy's introduction is that, although the Seventy are not mentioned again in Luke's Gospel, they presage the emergence of other appointed "sent ones" outside of the Twelve in Luke's second volume. It may be argued that both Barnabas and Paul, each in his own way, stand in a line of extra-apostolic "sent ones" that finds its origin with the Seventy. And so, having set the stage, we can at last turn our attention to the key players in our drama.

The Curtain Rises

After a brief word about how I approach the book of Acts, we move to chapter 1, where we explore how the two characters first emerge almost as afterthoughts at the end of two respective chapters in Acts. They appear and then disappear again, like character actors who capture your imagination, though they are not listed on the marquee out front. And yet, their quiet introductions, starting with the moment when they first meet, simply set up the plot twists that emerge later. It is particularly interesting to see how their initial debuts contrast with each other. Barnabas is immediately welcomed by the inner circle in Jerusalem, who take note of his generous and encouraging spirit. Paul, on the other hand, is suspect from the start because of his earlier persecution of followers of Jesus. And yet we see how he is far more "dangerous" after his conversion, and how Barnabas is his (quiet) revolutionary model.

Chapter 2 sets up another contrast, this time between two cities so important in the life of the early church. We witness the success that the Jesus movement enjoys in Jerusalem, but we also see the limits of that success and just how difficult it is for the insider community to look beyond themselves to those they consider outsiders. The tale of the Roman centurion Cornelius is examined as a great example of reluctant acceptance of God's larger plan, and is immediately contrasted with the enthusiastic embracing of outsiders in the emerging community in Antioch. And in one of the most monumental yet underrated verses of the entire New Testament, we learn the significance of a name.

Chapter 3 focuses on how the community in Antioch moves beyond the official leadership roles and gives a whole new meaning to apostleship. We see Paul's own role shift and change, from Barnabas's apprentice to peer to senior partner. And with new understandings of apostleship, we also see the beginnings of opposition to Paul as a leader. This leads us to examine how in his own letters, Paul develops new and exciting ways of expressing what it means to be a Christian community, while also fighting tooth and nail for his own position of leadership in that system.

In chapter 4, we move beyond the comfortable Jewish roots of the early Christian movement and begin to see the impact of Greek thought and Roman structure on the evolving church. The interweaving of old and new results in some dangerous moments for Barnabas and Paul in Acts, and presages the long-term struggle between honoring the past and accommodating the new and unfamiliar, a struggle that persists into our own time.

Chapter 5 shows how the circumcision issue becomes the catalyst for the great battle between old and new, insider and outsider. The resolution of that issue at the Jerusalem Council literally changes the course of history. Yet, unsurprisingly, some of those involved still cling to the former ways. Here we see through his own words the strength of Paul's convictions about the equalizing power of the Christian gospel, as well as the depth of his disappointment in Peter and, even more, in his colleague Barnabas.

In chapter 6, we come to perhaps the most pervasive indictment against Paul—that he was a misogynist and initiated policies that led to the suppression of women for centuries. Here, contrary to the images that have been propagated for centuries, we consider a very different picture of the apostle, who like his mentor became an encourager in relation to women, as seen in passages in both Acts and Paul's own letters.

In chapter 7, we see how Paul has often been described as socially conservative in regards to issues of sexuality, power, and slavery, a supporter of the status quo. But in the face of his imprisonment and approaching probable death, the apostle proves to be a strong advocate for a young runaway slave, and offers an argument that sounds very much like something Barnabas might have said on his own behalf years before. The result is the tiny epistle to Philemon, potentially a powerful manifesto against social disparities in a Christian community.

The conclusion returns to important questions about stereotyping. How did Paul gain a reputation so very different from what Acts and his own undisputed writings seem to say about him? How did the leader who opposed Barnabas precisely because the latter did *not* stand up for those in need become known instead as the reactionary who held back the revolutionary power of the Christian gospel? As with Dostoyevsky's classic tale of "The Grand Inquisitor," we consider the principle that when the church cannot condemn or kill a leader who upsets the equilibrium, it rather moves to canonize the individual and control his image (as with Paul) or push him off into relative obscurity (as with Barnabas).

As a denouement, we have an appendix on "The Barnabas Principle," a practical approach for congregational development, using the name *Barnabas* as an acronym with eight clear steps, all grounded in the life and ministry of the Great Encourager himself as found in Acts.

By exploring their common journey in the pages that follow, it is hoped that we can move beyond myths and assumptions and reclaim the legacies of an encourager most don't remember and an apostle many don't like.

Theirs was a partnership that, quite literally, changed the world.

It's time to find out why.

Discussion Questions

1. What were your impressions of Barnabas and Paul before opening this book? What assumptions about Paul have you accepted as true? Why do you think this book is called *Barnabas vs. Paul*? How do you think they differed?

2. How does Jesus in Luke's Gospel display a true availability and ac-

cessibility to his followers? How do the apostles show both positive and negative examples of leadership in Luke's Gospel?

3. What kind of leadership do you see in your own church or faith community? If "a leader leads," who would you designate as your leaders, both official (i.e., clergy, appointed lay leaders) and unofficial (i.e., individuals who display the kind of available and accessible leadership mentioned above)?

4. Why might it be difficult for Christians, both in the past and today, to acknowledge some failures on the part of the original apostles? How do we put our own leaders on a pedestal? How do we respond when they fall?

5. James and John were angry about the outsider who was casting out demons in Jesus's name—"he isn't in our group of followers."[32] Who are the successful outsiders in our own situation whom we either resent or fear? What can we learn from these outsiders that might strengthen our own ministry? How might we reach out to them, instead of pushing them away?

Chapter 1

Dangerous Newcomers

Moving beyond First Impressions

The great directors of stage and screen thrillers—those masters of suspense—somehow always find a way to surprise you in the end. When the guilty party is finally unmasked, it is never the one you imagined all along. In fact, as the familiar adage goes, it's usually "the one you least suspect." So much for first impressions! When Barnabas makes his debut at the end of Acts 4, he appears to be the ultimate "nice guy," a generous, encouraging, supportive follower who helps promote stability in the Jerusalem community. Paul, on the other hand, when introduced at the end of Acts 7 (with his Hebrew name, Saul), seems to be the obvious "bad guy," an angry, cruel, vengeful persecutor who spreads fear and dread among the followers of Jesus. Such first impressions would be quite misleading, as Barnabas and Paul are much more than they initially appear to be. Indeed, each in their own way will turn out to be far more dangerous than either the apostles or the outside world could imagine.

Second Impressions: The Witnesses

But before we pull back the curtain, we have one more task to ensure that the stage is properly set and ready for Barnabas's and Paul's entrances. In Luke 9 we got our first impressions of the Twelve, as they were commissioned for ministry and we saw how, just one chapter later, another group—the Seventy—was likewise commissioned, at least in part because of the Twelve's

15

inadequacies. Now, at the beginning of Acts the Twelve get a second chance and we get to form our second impressions of them following the events of Jesus's death and resurrection, as the Twelve receive a new commission from the risen Christ, complete with Spirit-filled empowerment. This second commission, this Great Commission, tells them what they are called to be, and where they are called to go.

And so, we make our way to the opening verses in the first chapter of Acts, to a mountain where the resurrected Jesus is preparing to take his leave, and where a final conversation with his apostles ensues. The conversation begins with a seemingly innocent question on their part: "Are you going to restore the kingdom to Israel now?"[1] On one level their question is understandable, given that Israel's restoration under a warrior-king like David a millennia before was an ongoing hope for many around them. Indeed, many would-be messiahs were running around in Jesus's time. Given that their mentor has now somehow defeated death itself, the apostles understandably assume that a new golden age for Israel is about to be born. To show how serious they are, they spend the rest of Acts 1 involved in the selection of a twelfth apostle to take the place of the now departed betrayer, Judas Iscariot, so that their number might once again represent the twelve tribes of ancient Israel.[2]

And yet Jesus's response to the apostles reveals how off-target their question is. The apostles are ready to see their risen Lord usher in a new golden age for Israel, but Jesus counters with a broader, deeper Commission: "It isn't for you to know the times or seasons that the Father has set by his own authority. Rather, you will receive power when the Holy Spirit has come upon you, and you will be my witnesses in Jerusalem, in all Judea and Samaria, and to the end of the earth."[3] It is the Great Commission according to Luke, both similar to, and distinct from, the more oft-quoted version from the end of Matthew's Gospel: "I've received all authority in heaven and on earth. Therefore, go and make disciples of all nations, baptizing them in the name of the Father and of the Son and of the Holy Spirit, teaching them to obey everything that I've commanded you. Look, I myself will be with you every day until the end of this present age."[4]

Both versions of the Commission speak of divine empowerment and both express a call to action. God's mission, both then and now, is not intended to be a spectator sport. Neither they nor we can opt to sit in the stands and simply watch. "Go and make disciples," Jesus cries out in Matthew.[5] "You will be my witnesses," he asserts in Acts.[6] This word *witnesses* is particularly interesting, and to understand its significance, it's helpful to dust off the old Greek texts and explore the word's origin. The Greek *martyroi* literally translates to "martyrs." All too often, we think of martyrs as those who face death for the sake of a greater cause, people such as Dr. Martin Luther King Jr. or Archbishop Oscar Romero of El Salvador. And in a less noble context, most of us have heard people at times describe as martyrs those who grudgingly take on tasks or responsibilities that they really don't want: "Oh, she's just being a martyr!" or "He has such a martyr complex." But at its heart, being a martyr means bearing witness to something, as if in a court of law. The prohibition, "You shall not bear false witness against your neighbor," is part of the Decalogue, the Ten Commandments. Jesus calls the apostles to be *true* witnesses, *bold* witnesses, *empowered* witnesses, of all that they have seen and experienced. Their actions as well as their words should point beyond themselves not simply to the restoration of a glorious past but to the promise of a glorious destiny, abundant life in Christ for all the world.

When I was in college, cancer struck my close friend Don. People around him prayed for recovery, but the cancer grew and spread. As others either denied the inevitable or shook their fists towards heaven, Don just carried on with a smile on his face and a kind word to those around him. Toward the end, when friends came to comfort him, they left his room speaking with astonishment of the comfort he gave to them, of how he prayed for them. After his passing, the church where his funeral was held was filled to capacity. The person next to me was a nurse who only knew him in his final months through his chemotherapy treatments. Yet there she was because, as she said, she had seen something in him that changed her. Don was a martyr in the truest sense, both in his death but even more in his life. He exemplified what Francis of Assisi is rumored to have once said: "Preach the gospel at all times; if necessary use words."

And so, there on the mountain, Jesus appoints the apostles to be his martyrs, his empowered witnesses. And where are they supposed to fulfill this Commission? In Jerusalem, the very place to which their Lord had set his face back in Luke 9, the very place where he went on to face arrest and death. Yes, Jerusalem is the focal point of their mission, but at the same time Jesus's Commission to them makes it clear that it is also to be the *starting point* from which they must go, to paraphrase the author C. S. Lewis, "further up and further out"[7]—out to surrounding Judea, out to the despised and once-resistant Samaria, and ultimately out to the ends of the earth. When Jesus had earlier sent them out back in Luke 9, there was no mention of the geographical trajectory of their mission. Now there is. With each step outward, they are being called to a deeper trust and a broader vision, to get out of their boat and step into the unknown.

Do the apostles understand? Do they get it? This, unfortunately, is not at all clear. In Acts 2, the newly reconstituted Twelve (having selected Matthias to replace Judas), along with Mary and the faithful women who supported Jesus's ministry, and other unnamed friends, together experience the fulfillment of Jesus's promise of divine empowerment. Like a rushing wind, the Holy Spirit bursts through their sealed room and they are transformed. Empowered by the Spirit, the previously frightened apostles themselves burst through the doors in order to proclaim the greatness of God and of Jesus the Christ to all who will listen. And many do listen, devout Jews in Jerusalem for Pentecost, the second of the great Jewish feasts. Celebrated fifty days after Passover, when a lamb was sacrificed and first-fruits were offered, Pentecost pointed to the fullness of what was foreseen in the first-fruits seven weeks previously with the presentation of new grain from the harvest on Pentecost.[8] More than this, Pentecost commemorated the giving of the Decalogue at Mount Sinai, the Mosaic Law that would help form the basis of the community that had proceeded out of Egypt. Unlike Passover, which was intended to be a more private, family commemoration, Pentecost was an opportunity for the people to come together for a brief time to renew their connection to God and to one another, to recall the ties of both liberty and law that bind them as one.

Thus, faithful Jews from all parts of the Roman Empire find themselves on this particular Pentecost listening to a small group of emboldened apostles bear witness to Jesus as the promised Messiah, hearing the words in their own languages, like a reversal of the curse of Babel, when understanding gave way to confusion and babbling. The Pentecost miracle reverses all that, as the crowd hears in their own native tongues the proclamation of the Twelve and asks, "Are not all these who are speaking Galileans?"[9] Luke notes that three thousand believe and are baptized—a very successful day indeed. And in the days that follow, there are repeated instances of proclamation[10] and power.[11] As far as *second* impressions go, following their empowerment by the Spirit, the Twelve appear to be fulfilling Jesus's Commission quite well; they have come a long way from their earlier inadequacies in Luke's Gospel.

There is just one problem. All the preaching and miraculous signs of the Twelve, indeed all their success in those early chapters of Acts, occur solely in Jerusalem, in the very shadow of the temple. Yes, thousands respond to the apostles' message on Pentecost, but the converts are all Jews or Jewish prose- lytes. Yes, the Twelve help form a community of love and sharing, but they still spend time each day in the temple prayers, and presumably the sacrifices. The healing of a lame man occurs at the "Beautiful Gate" as Peter and John are going "up to the temple at the hour of prayer."[12] Peter addresses the people at Solomon's Portico, and after their release from the authorities, the Twelve return daily to the temple. And later in Acts 8, as a result of the persecution following the death of Stephen, Luke explicitly states that all the followers of Jesus are scattered throughout Judea and Samaria—all, that is, except for the Twelve. Having once been told to wait in the city,[13] the Twelve do just that! They preach and heal, they enjoy great success, but all of it is in the familiar environs of Jerusalem. They believe that Jesus is the Messiah, the Christ, but they remain a Jewish sect, an insiders' club. It is as if the new wine of the gospel remains held in the old wineskin of their familiar religious traditions.

How many times have our own churches become insiders' clubs? There is an old joke that says that everyone who should be an Episcopalian (or name your denomination) already is one! Newcomers might be welcome, but only as long as they look and sound like us. How comforting it is to experience growth and energy as long as we don't have to really change. Like a thermo- stat or a car's cruise control, small deviations from the norm are allowed, as long as the system eventually returns to normal. Like the apostles, we can easily remain in the shadow of the temple, never leaving our comfort zone. To move further out, to move beyond Jerusalem to the ends of the earth, we need someone to assist, someone with a foot in both the world we know and the world beyond, someone who can build a bridge and help us take our first steps into the unknown.

First Impressions: The Encourager

Barnabas is first introduced on Luke's stage at the end of a passage that describes the intentional sharing of possessions among Jesus's followers.

> The community of believers was one in heart and mind. None of them would say, "This is mine!" about any of their possessions, but held everything in common. The apostles continued to bear powerful witness to the resurrection of the Lord Jesus, and an abundance of grace was at work among them all. There were no needy persons among them. Those who owned properties or houses would sell them, bring the proceeds from the sales, and place them in the care and under the authority of the apostles. Then it was distributed to anyone who was in need. Joseph, whom the apostles nicknamed Barnabas (that is, "one who encourages"), was a Levite from Cyprus. He owned a field, sold it, brought the money, and placed it in the care and under the authority of the apostles.[14]

This initial mention of Barnabas is a modest one, naming him as one among many who generously donates money from a property sale for the good of the community of believers, laying the proceeds at the feet of the apostles. In this brief introduction, however, a lot may be learned about him, beginning with his generosity. In icons made of Barnabas he is often pictured holding a money bag, ready to give it away. Luke himself stresses his munificence, contrasting Barnabas with the miserly, deceitful couple, Ananias and Sapphira, whose grim tale depicts them holding back proceeds from the apostles and lying about it. Their meanness of spirit only makes Barnabas's bigheartedness that much more impressive.

As a brief interlude, it is important to step back and recognize that throughout Luke's Gospel and Acts people who experience a conversion in their lives often reflect that internal change by reordering their financial priorities. An obvious example found in Luke 19 is the tale of Zaccheus, that delightful, vertically-challenged tax collector who climbs a sycamore tree just to be able to see Jesus. He is Luke's model of a converted life. There is no mention in his tale of reciting a creedal statement or undergoing an initiation rite. What Luke records instead is that following Jesus's visit to his house, Zaccheus immediately pledges to recompense those he has cheated . . . fourfold!

Like Zaccheus, Barnabas gives freely, without reservation, for the good of the community. This is more than just almsgiving, that tangible form of compassion exemplified in both the Psalms—"Those who pay close attention to the poor are truly happy!"[15]—and Proverbs—"Those who exploit the powerless anger their maker, / while those who are kind to the poor honor God."[16] While he offers several examples of Zaccheus-like people whose converted lives are precisely evident in their almsgiving—people like Tabitha of Joppa, Cornelius the God-fearing centurion, and Paul himself[17]—Luke moves beyond almsgiving in describing the financial choices made by the apostles and their community after the events of Pentecost. The new converts immediately begin to display a radical change in life: "All the believers were united and shared everything. They would sell pieces of property and possessions and distribute the proceeds to everyone who needed them."[18] As already noted, an almost identical tale is related in Acts 4, suggesting that, for Luke, Pentecost was not simply a one-time event, but rather an ongoing experience among the Jerusalem believers:

> The community of believers was one in heart and mind. None of them would say, "This is mine!" about any of their possessions, but held everything in common. The apostles continued to bear powerful witness to the resurrection of the Lord Jesus, and an abundance of grace was at work among them all. There were no needy persons among them. Those who owned properties or houses would sell them, bring the proceeds from the sales, and place them in the care and under the authority of the apostles. Then it was distributed to anyone who was in need.[19]

This kind of giving goes beyond general almsgiving, beyond what is usually called "outreach" in today's churches, for the recipients of financial help here are fellow members of the community itself. Here, it is not Psalm 41 or Proverbs 14 that provide Old Testament precedents, but rather Deuteronomy 15: "If there are some poor persons among you, say one of your fellow Israelites . . . don't be hard-hearted or tightfisted toward your poor fellow Israelites."[20] Leviticus 25 similarly states: "If one of your fellow Israelites faces financial difficulty and is in a shaky situation with you, you must assist them."[21] The most powerful and visible argument for the truths the apostles proclaimed was not the deeds of power that accompanied their message, but rather Luke's claim that there was not a needy person among them. Miracles astound and amaze, but a community that truly takes care of its own is particularly attractive, whether then or today. The second-century Christian leader Justin Martyr would similarly proclaim: "We who once coveted . . . the wealth of others now place in common the goods we possess."[22]

What Luke and Justin report was not unknown in the ancient world. Over three centuries before the coming of Christ, Aristotle quoted the proverbial saying, "Friends' goods are common property," commenting that even as members of a family hold "all things in common," so do members of a close community.[23] The Jewish historian Jospehus provides perhaps the most fascinating analogy to the Christians' communal approach to finances in his account of another first-century Jewish sect, the Essenes: "They have a law that new members on admission to the sect shall confiscate their property to the order, with the result that you will nowhere see either abject poverty or inordinate wealth; the individual's possessions join the common stock and all, like members of the same family, enjoy a single patrimony."[24] Josephus's high regard for the Essenes is clear—"their community of goods is truly admirable"—and perhaps overly idealistic.[25] As will be seen momentarily, Luke is far more honest about the not-so-idyllic reality of the Jerusalem church. For now, however, let's return to that one particular donor in Jerusalem who catches the apostles' attention.

Again, Luke says that Barnabas sells a field and brings the proceeds from that sale in full, placing them in the care and under the authority of the apostles. A literal and perhaps more accurate translation of the original Greek, found in the New Revised Standard Version and other English versions, is "laying them at the feet of the apostles."[26] This last detail is important. The phrase "at the feet" is a significant one for Luke, who uses it to denote a sense of devotion or reverence that the giver has for the recipient as well as the trustworthiness of that recipient. It is a phrase found most often in Luke's Gospel and Acts; indeed, over forty-three percent of all New Testament occurrences of "feet" occur in his two volumes. Perhaps this evangelist often referred to as "the physician" should be known as Luke the podiatrist! The Fourth Gospel also makes use of "feet," but usually in the symbolic context of service, for example, the anointing of Jesus's feet by the "sinful" woman and the washing of the disciples' feet by Jesus himself.[27] Luke instead focuses on the reverential theme of individuals at the feet of Jesus: to listen to him teach (the Gerasene demoniac, and Mary the sister of Martha); to seek help from him (Jairus); to offer thanks for healing already received (the Samaritan leper).[28] In each case, the imagery of being at the feet of Jesus clearly conveys a sense of deep devotion. This sense of devotion is also found in Acts, most notably in the story of the centurion Cornelius who prostrates himself at the feet of Peter, and in Paul's comment that he had once studied "under Gamiliel's instruction" or, as in other translations of the Greek, "at the feet of Gamiliel."[29]

However, "at the feet" is also used in Acts to denote the entrusting of possessions to another who is deemed trustworthy, as when the witnesses at Stephen's stoning "placed their cloaks in the care of a young man named Saul," or again as translated in other versions, "laid their coats at the feet of a young man named Saul."[30] Both trust and respect are conveyed in the twin instances of followers laying their money at the feet of the apostles in Acts 4. The apostles exercise both spiritual and temporal leadership in the communal system. Under their leadership, the gospel message is preached *and* the needs of all in the community are met through the distribution of funds. Whatever the details of the allocation process, it is to the apostles that financial gifts such as Barnabas's are entrusted, and it is under their authority that distribution is made.[31]

For now, we see that Barnabas is one of a group of followers who sell what they own, give the proceeds through a system in some way involving the leadership of the Twelve, and in doing so exhibit a deep sense of their mutual interdependence. Some, including the second-century Clement of Alexandria, claim he was one of the Seventy.[32] When the English translation of Acts 4 declares that the believers were "of one heart and mind,"[33] what is actually said in the original Greek is that "there was one heart and soul in the multitude of those who believed." This is more than a common purpose: It is a common life. Both Barnabas and his many unnamed companions show

23

that they are stewards not simply of money, but of one another. But there is much more to learn.

We note that Barnabas is a Levite, a descendent of the priestly tribe of Israel. He is not, however, a priest himself, at least not in the sense of having duties in the Jerusalem temple. He is, in fact, not from Jerusalem at all, but rather is a native of Cyprus in the Mediterranean, part of the Jewish Diaspora. This means that unlike Peter and the other Palestinian-based apostles whose primary spoken language was Aramaic, Barnabas's would have been Greek. Likewise, he most likely would have read the scriptures not in the original Hebrew, but rather in the Greek translation known to us as the Septuagint.[34] Nevertheless, he bears a familiar Jewish name, Joseph, the name of that most famous of Israel's sons, the dreamer with the coat of many colors who was sold into slavery yet rose to become a leader in Egypt. Like his namesake, this newcomer to the apostolic community appears to be destined for great things, marked out by the Twelve not just for his generosity with money but also for his generous spirit toward others. It is they who bestow upon this newcomer the nickname by which he would henceforth be known, so that Joseph of Cyprus becomes Barnabas, the "son of encouragement."

From this brief debut, our first impressions of Barnabas might well be similar to that which the Twelve clearly had of him: someone who is likeable, supportive, and trustworthy. They—and we—are right about all that, of course. But look just a little more closely and see that, unlike the apostles, Barnabas is a property owner, a person of some means, as well as a Cyprian, not a Palestinian, an outsider who presumably has seen more of the world than they. The Twelve are right to respect and trust Barnabas, but make no mistake. At their bidding, this generous newcomer, possibly one of the Seventy, will eventually take on an ambassadorial role to another community of believers in another city and in the process irreversibly change everything.

First Impressions: The Persecutor

If the first impression that Luke gives of Barnabas is positive, take note of the contrasting image of Paul when we first encounter him:

Once the council members heard these words, they were enraged and began to grind their teeth at Stephen. But Stephen, enabled by the Holy Spirit, stared into heaven and saw God's majesty and Jesus standing at God's right side. He exclaimed, "Look! I can see heaven on display and the Human One standing at God's right side!" At this, they shrieked and covered their ears. Together, they charged at him, threw him out of the city, and began to stone him. The witnesses placed their coats in the care of a young man named Saul. As they battered him with stones, Stephen prayed, "Lord Jesus, accept my life!" Falling to his knees, he shouted, "Lord, don't hold this sin against them!" Then he died.[35]

As with Barnabas's debut, it is important to consider the context in which Paul is introduced, standing off to the side of the stage at the climactic moment of Stephen's martyrdom. To understand the significance of this, it is important to step back once more and take note of the change that had begun to take place in the life of the Jerusalem community at the start of Acts 6. "About that time," Luke says, "while the number of disciples continued to increase, a complaint arose. Greek-speaking disciples accused the Aramaic-speaking disciples because their widows were being overlooked in the daily food service."[36] The descriptors used here by Luke—"Greek-speaking disciples" and "Aramaic-speaking disciples," or as described in other translations, "Hellenists" and "Hebrews"—might well leave readers today with more ambiguity than clarity regarding both the exact nature of the conflict and the identity of the players involved.[37] The Greek-speaking disciples likely come from somewhere outside Palestine, like Barnabas of Cyprus, but in any case it is clear is that this is not a case of outside agitators; the dispute is *within* the boundaries of the apostolic community.[38] In Acts 4, it was said that everything was held in common and distribution was made so that no one was in need. Two chapters later, the Greek speakers complain that this is not happening for their widows.

And what is the apostles' response to the complaints brought before them? They declare that their duties are to pray and preach, not "serve tables." Instead, they challenge the complaining Greek-speaking disciples to choose seven men from among their own number to fulfill the task of distribution. They do so, and seven men, all with Greek names, are chosen and then appointed by the Twelve. Luke says that the entire group approves the decision, and many since then have seen it was a wise move and an extension of the ministry of the Twelve. But is it not possible that Luke is suggesting something else? After all, the Twelve were quite willing to oversee distribution issues earlier, in Acts 4 and 5, as proceeds from property sales were laid at their feet. Now, as the community is growing and also growing more diverse, one subset consisting of non-Palestinian Jewish followers of Jesus is feeling neglected. And the Twelve essentially distance themselves from it, instead giving over the task to insiders of that subset. In the short term, it solves the immediate problem, but in the long run, do not the actions of the Twelve actually perpetuate the distinction between the two groups? How many times have we found ways to perpetuate the boundaries between people, often using some variation of the formula "separate but equal" to provide short-term solutions to real or potential conflict between groups? How often have we let our own fears prevent us from being truly welcoming?

Whatever the answer to these questions, the fact is that Luke has introduced yet another numbered group for the work of mission. The Seven in Acts 6, like the Seventy in Luke 10, are raised up to do what the Twelve either cannot or will not do. And, like the Seventy, the Seven (at least in the persons of Stephen and Philip) also take on the same task of proclamation as the Twelve . . . with one crucial difference. While Peter and the others retain their custom of daily prayer and worship at the temple, Stephen instead challenges the very need for the temple in what is the single longest sermon in the book of Acts. "The Most High doesn't live in houses built by human hands," Stephen declares.[39] The result is ugly . . . and, for Stephen, deadly. And this is where Paul comes into the picture, a young man on the sidelines, holding the cloaks of the enraged men with rocks in their hands and hatred in their hearts.

What do we know of Paul's life before this debut? Acts later says that that he studied under Gamiliel's instruction, a leading rabbi noted for his wisdom and tolerance. It was this same Gamiliel who called for a moderate response on the part of the religious leaders in Jerusalem toward Peter and the other apostles, arguing that this new movement would probably die out on its own. But if it was of divine origin, he warned, they may even be found fighting against God. It was under such an astute mentor that Paul studied, and he soon became a rising rabbinic scholar in his own right. From his own letters we learn that Paul advanced beyond many of his peers largely because of his zeal for the traditions of his ancestors. He was proud of his ancestry and his faith. Like Barnabas, Paul—also known by his Hebrew name, Saul—could trace his ancestry back to the tribe of Benjamin, much like his namesake from a thousand years before, Israel's first king.

Although he would describe himself a "Hebrew of Hebrews," Paul, or *Paulus* in Latin, was also intensely proud of his Roman citizenship, and apparently well versed in the poetry and philosophy of the Greek and Roman world. Whether it was the result of meritorious service done by his parents or some other reason, Paul was born a Roman citizen, a rare honor for one of the occupied peoples in Palestine. He was, in truth, a man of two worlds, with an impressive pedigree in each. How then did this rising star become known as a persecutor, chasing down a motley crew of sectarians, especially when his own mentor seemed to follow a more lenient course?

Like a good mystery story, the answer just might be hiding in plain sight. Gamiliel had encountered disciples like Peter and John who showed every sign of being faithful to their Jewish heritage, worshipping daily in the temple, as well as respectful of surrounding Roman customs and laws. Paul faced a different kind of follower in the more radical Hellenist, Stephen. To Peter and his colleagues, Jesus was the one who would one day restore the kingdom to Israel, so they had little reason to move beyond the shadow of the temple or provoke their Roman occupiers. To Stephen, on the other hand, Jesus changed everything, thereby making the temple—and all that it represented in terms of the religious and social boundaries between Jews and non-Jews—irrelevant. There is an irony here. Paul was a man of two worlds, at once the Roman *Paulus* and also the Hebrew Saul, yet he kept these worlds separate and distinct. The danger to Paul in Stephen's message was a blurring of important boundaries on which ancient Israel's very existence depended. In Jesus, there is neither Jew nor Greek. Stephen understood this, and was thereby a threat to the status quo, a threat to Israel's very existence. For the young man Saul, Stephen's stoning is neither a hate crime nor a martyrdom; it is an execution for a dangerous traitor. And so he dutifully watches over the cloaks entrusted to him, laid at his feet much like the money earlier entrusted to the apostles by Barnabas and others. Saul/Paul grasps what Peter and the others did not seem to comprehend, that Jesus breaks down boundaries and shatters the status quo and is thereby quite dangerous and potentially so are all those who follow him.

This same Saul then sets out on the road from Jerusalem to Damascus, to try to bring an end to what he sees as a dangerous movement, only to face what he dreaded. With a blinding light and a fall to the ground, he hears the heavenly voice: "Saul, Saul, why are you harassing me?" "Who are you, Lord?" he asks, only to hear the very answer he dreads hearing: "I am Jesus, whom you are harrassing."[40] As he would often remind both friends and opponents alike in later years, Paul's encounter with Jesus was no less real, no less authentic than Peter's or any of the other apostles'. He may not have walked with Jesus for three years as they did, but he met him on the road to Damascus and would be forever changed as a result. Blinded by the experience and led by the hand into the city, for three days Paul is buried in darkness, until a disciple named Ananias (different from the deceitful member of the Jerusalem community in Acts 5) baptizes him and his eyes are opened to a whole new life. Of course, at first Ananias is reluctant to do this, even as the Twelve are reluctant even to meet with Paul when he comes to Jerusalem to see them. For Paul, the strong negative first impressions people had of him would be difficult to overcome.

And this is where Barnabas reenters the stage. Five chapters after being introduced, the Encourager brings the intimidating newcomer before the apostles and personally vouches for him. It's ironic really. The Twelve are nervous about Saul/Paul because he has persecuted followers of Jesus. Saul/Paul has persecuted followers of Jesus because he saw how one of them, Stephen, threatened to break down the social and religious boundaries that supported the status quo and kept outsiders at arm's length. Stephen only came to prominence because the Twelve had been reluctant to personally deal with the complaints of Greek speakers who felt like outsiders in the apostolic community. And Barnabas the Cyprian, a Hellenist, an outsider, who once earned the respect and trust of the Twelve, now taps into that respect and trust to vouch for the one they fear. Because of Barnabas, the former persecutor of the faith would go on to become its greatest proponent. Together Barnabas and

Paul would move beyond Jerusalem, and beyond others' first impressions, as bold witnesses of the gospel of life and liberation, to the very destination to which Jesus had once called the Twelve, the ends of the earth.

Discussion Questions

1. What does the word *martyr* mean to you? Who are some people who have been God's bold witnesses in your life?

2. Pentecost is one of the major feasts of the church, but what does it mean to you? If you were going to explain to a congregation why it is important to celebrate it, what would you say to convince them?

3. Barnabas displays both generosity with material possessions and generosity of spirit towards others. What holds you back from being radically generous, either with possessions or with encouragement?

4. The apostles made a decision to turn over their responsibility for distribution issues to Stephen and the other Greek-speaking leaders. Why is this problematic? What are the roles of clergy and lay leaders in a congregation? When should they share responsibility and when should they take on different responsibilities?

5. The leaders of the Jerusalem community had a negative first impression of Saul/Paul. When have you been wrong in your opinion about someone? How does your church respond to different types of newcomers?

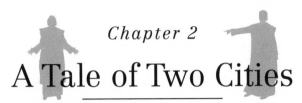

Chapter 2

A Tale of Two Cities

Moving beyond the Insider Community

M ake no mistake: growth means headaches. The attractiveness of the status quo is precisely that it is familiar, predictable, manageable. How often have I met with congregational leaders and heard them express their strong desire for new members. I usually respond, only slightly tongue-in-cheek, "I don't believe you!" I say this because I know that growth almost always means some kind of change to the system, especially if the new members include families with children (who aren't always quiet!) or newcomers with radically different backgrounds or opinions than the existing membership. At first glance, an increase in numbers and financial giving sounds so appealing to congregational leaders—at least until I begin to explore with them the implications of these outsiders for their familiar, predictable, manageable, insider community. It is then that the nervous coughs and squirming in the seats begin.

None of this is new, by the way. In the previous chapter, we saw how it was precisely when the disciples were growing in number that problems began to emerge between the insiders and the newcomers in their midst. As long as the apostolic community in Jerusalem remained a largely Palestinian-Jewish sectarian movement, a subset of a subset in the Roman Empire, as long as they stayed firmly in one place—there in the shadow of the temple—the community's potential for growth, both numerically and in terms of any kind of diversity, was destined to hit a ceiling. Despite Peter's assurances in his

Pentecost address that the message of salvation was open to "everyone who calls on the name of the Lord," his words were clearly addressed to "fellow Israelites" gathered for the great feast, his sermon filled with quotations from the Hebrew scriptures.[1] Peter was preaching to the choir, as it were.

Likewise, while it is impressive to read of the communal sharing that marked the apostolic community in the earliest period, the events in Acts 6 imply that it was at least partly due to the relative homogeneity of its membership before the group's growth spurt. More people meant more demands on finite resources, but more people *who were new and different* meant that inherent biases were likely to arise when facing demands on finite resources. Financial support understandably stayed "in the family," so when Luke speaks of the Hellenists', or Greek-speaking disciples', complaint about their widows being neglected, it is as if he is suggesting that, though they had been accepted into the family, they clearly were being treated as unwelcome "stepchildren." That tale about inequitable pastoral care is a reminder that even in those earliest days, when the believers were seemingly "of one heart and mind,"[2] they still struggled to find a way to integrate and fully include those among them who were different. After all, it was one thing to have Barnabas of Cyprus around—the supportive, generous donor—but real problems emerged when outsiders arrived in far greater numbers.

And some seemed to be looking for trouble. Before, even when they were going daily to the temple as faithful devotees, Peter and his fellow apostles found themselves in hot water with religious authorities suspicious of these sectarians. Along comes Stephen, one of those appointed to deal with the Greek speakers' complaints to make things easier for the Twelve. Instead, here he is stirring up trouble, questioning the very need for the temple, which simply provokes anger against them all. Harassment turns into outright persecution. Many of the believers move out of Jerusalem, unwittingly fulfilling Jesus's Commission. And some of these make their way to a city called Antioch.

A World Apart

For Luke, as for many of the biblical authors, places matter. They are more than just background sets. Two thousand years ago, as today, Jerusalem was a place of profound devotion and intense emotion. As Luke notes in his Gospel, Jerusalem is the goal toward which Jesus sets his face and moves inexorably despite his apostles' fearful protests. With his penchant for plot twists and reversals, Luke shows how their eventual arrival is met not with an immediate assault on Jesus, but rather with popular support, as people cheer and palms are laid on the ground like an ancient red carpet for the triumphant heir-apparent to King David's throne. Still, Jesus moves on to the city's center, to its very heart, the temple where heaven and earth meet and humanity is reconciled to God. Again, Luke offers a twist. In the midst of all the wonderful, hopeful celebrations, Jesus violently overthrows tables and shouts out diatribes, incurring the wrath of the religious authorities and the anxiety of the Roman overseers. Jerusalem becomes the site of Jesus's greatest challenge as well as his ultimate victory. And as we have seen in the first few chapters of Acts, it also becomes home base for the apostles. When many among their community find themselves dispersed throughout the Roman Empire following Stephen's death, the Twelve stay put, there in that familiar city where they could proclaim Jesus while remaining connected to their Jewish roots, there in the shadow of the temple.

Antioch of Syria, on the other hand, was a world apart from Jerusalem. While the latter was considered by non-Jews as little more than the backwaters of the Roman Empire, overseen by second-rate bureaucrats such as Pontius Pilate, Antioch was one of the empire's largest and most important cities.[3] By the time of Barnabas and Paul, the city was three centuries old, founded by the Syrian ruler Seleucus Nicator, a former general under Alexander the Great, and named for Seleucus's father Antiochus.[4] The city's commercially strategic location on a caravan route across land from Persia to the navigable waters of the Orontes River and leading down to the Mediterranean Sea ensured both a thriving trade and a cosmopolitan feel. Well over half a million people of diverse cultures and dialects crossed paths with one another on a daily basis. In 64 BCE, Rome annexed Antioch and it soon ranked third in both size and importance in the empire, just behind Rome and Alexandria. It would remain in this top tier for centuries, until the eventual rise of an upstart city named Constantinople. In the first century, Jerusalem was clearly an occupied city overseen by a series of reluctant bureaucrats such as Pontius Pilate. Antioch, on the other hand, was a thoroughly Hellenistic and Roman city, laid out in a grid patterns and full of government employees, impressive public works such as aqueducts and baths, popular (and often brutal) sporting events, and numerous theaters and other cultural outlets. At its annexation, the Roman general Pompey declared Antioch to be a "free city," and four decades later it was made the seat of the governor for the newly consolidated Roman province of Syria, which included, interestingly, Palestine.

Jerusalem was so clearly Jewish, dominated by Herod's temple, the so-called Second Temple, the original having been built by Solomon almost a millennium before, only then to be destroyed a few centuries later during the Babylonian conquest. Daily prayers and sacrifices continued to provide the rhythm of life, a rhythm that, as we have seen, the apostles and their followers fully embraced. Antioch, on the other hand, was a religious potpourri in which people worshipping different deities coexisted with one another. Roman rulers ordered the restoration of temples dedicated respectively to Artemis, Ares, Athena, and Zeus. Barely five miles away from Antioch was a major center of worship devoted to the goddess Daphne and her consort Apollo. Within the city, the robed goddess Tyche was especially beloved, owing to a great statue of her created around 300 BCE. Her visage appeared on coins during the Roman period, depicted with a sheaf of wheat in her hand, a crown on her head, and river deity Orontes at her feet. Some other mystery religions espoused more dubious practices such as "sacred prostitution," leading many in that time to bemoan Antioch's immorality as what we might today call a "sin city."

In the midst of this religious mix there also existed a sizeable Jewish community, dating back to the time of Seleucus I himself. Unlike their counterparts living in Jerusalem, many Antiochene Jews enjoyed financial stability and social mobility. They were able to hold onto their own faith without worrying about others bothering them; indeed, they seemed to given a significant amount of self-governance within the larger civic structures. When in Acts 6 Luke names the Hellenists chosen by the people and appointed by the apostles to deal with the distribution crisis, one of the seven, Nicholas, is specifically designated as being a Jewish proselyte from Antioch.[5] Undoubtedly he was but one of many who could claim that designation. It is little surprise, then, that in the dispersion of Jesus's followers following Stephen's martyrdom, one of their destinations of safe refuge would be Antioch of Syria. And what they did there would, quite literally, change the world.

But before we turn to that scene, we must pull back the curtain once more and shine the spotlight on one of the other principal characters in this drama, and recognize a bit of our own selves in his response to possible change.

Reluctant Hospitality

In my particular vocation, I no longer shepherd a single parish but instead visit various congregations throughout the country, and indeed in many places around the world. I usually go as the guest preacher or in some other official capacity, but many times I have the opportunity to attend the Sunday service incognito, as one more newcomer among many. I remember a particular church renowned both for the impressive quality of its liturgy and for the sheer size and beauty of its sanctuary. Indeed, tourists often came with cameras on hand to view the building, with no intention of participating in its worship. For my part, arriving early so that I could do some touring of my own before the Eucharist began, I eventually made my way to the area where they served coffee and tea, and, given the cold winter's day outside, proceeded to make myself a cup. I confess that I like more sugar than I should with my tea, but apparently I used more than my expected allotment that day as one of the hosts overseeing the beverage area began to admonish me for all the things I was doing wrong. Finally, she said quite plainly, "The drinks are for those attending service, not for tourists" to which I quietly but firmly responded that I was indeed planning to worship there that day but most likely not again.

Hospitality requires intentionality. It doesn't just happen. We must choose to be hospitable, and not simply with those who make the effort to prove themselves worthy of our attention and care. It is possible, and often the case, that we "welcome" visitors and newcomers to our churches in quite unwelcoming ways. In this, we stand in fairly impressive company, as two millennia ago the Apostle Peter was faced with the challenge of welcoming into the insider community that he and the other apostles had so carefully nurtured a whole new kind of convert: not simply a Greek-speaking Jew, but a dreaded Gentile.

Now those who argue that the Jerusalem leadership was indeed hospitable and open to change often point to the story of Peter and Cornelius in Acts 10. Does this not indeed present a very positive image of the leader of the Twelve embracing the nascent Gentile movement? After all, following the tales of Stephen's sermon and death in Acts 7, of the evangelization of an Ethiopian in Samaria by Philip (another member of the Seven) in Acts 8, and of Saul/Paul's conversion in the early parts of Acts 9, Peter finally moves again to the foreground of Luke's stage. After paralleling Jesus's own ministry in healing a paralyzed man and raising a young woman from the dead,[6] he then is involved in the conversion of Cornelius's household in Acts 10. And this is where things get interesting! As we have already seen, Luke is deliberate in the details he offers and in the prominence certain events receive in his account. This particular story is so prominent that it overshadows what comes next in Acts 11, namely the evangelization of the Gentiles in Antioch. Why does Luke give such time and space to Peter's tale, and what does it mean for us? Before we answer, let's review the story itself.

Following the miraculous raising to life again of a woman in the town of Joppa, on the banks of the Mediterranean, Simon Peter apparently stays on for a time, lodging with a man similarly named Simon, a tanner by trade. It is during this stay, and while Peter is hungry, that he has a vision of various kinds of meat forbidden to him laid out as a feast, and then hears God's voice commanding him to rise and eat. But Peter—whether confused or thinking this a divine test or simply being stubborn—refuses to eat what is spread before him because it is unclean by Jewish dietary laws. The heavenly reply counters such overly scrupulous behavior, "Never consider unclean what God has made pure."[7] Three times this occurs, and when the vision finally leaves him, it is just in time for Peter to see visitors coming to him with a most unexpected invitation. They relate that they were sent by Cornelius, a Roman centurion and friend of the Jewish people. This Cornelius had also experienced a vision in which God told him to send for Peter in order to hear the apostle share good news with him and his household. Peter follows the entourage and declares to his host upon coming to the front of the house, "You all realize that it is forbidden for a Jew to associate or visit with outsiders. However, God has shown me that I should never call

36

a person impure or unclean. For this reason, when you sent for me, I came without objection."[8]

Peter proceeds to tell Cornelius and his household about Jesus's life, death, and resurrection. He describes himself and his fellow apostles as God's chosen witnesses called to preach to the people. Then comes the surprise! While Peter is still speaking, the Holy Spirit somehow descends upon the Gentile listeners in much the same way that the Spirit once infused and empowered the Twelve and their followers in Jerusalem. Peter asks his companions how any of them can possibly withhold baptism from the group, given the Spirit's clear presence in their midst. When challenged about all this back in Jerusalem in the first part of Acts 11, Luke shows Peter relating almost verbatim the entire episode once again. At last the believers there admit that even the Gentiles have been enabled by God "to change their hearts and lives so that they might have new life."[9] It is quite a lengthy, detailed story, and Luke clearly is trying to convey something important. But we must avoid the obvious temptation to conclude that this lengthy, detailed tale is evidence that the Jerusalem leadership, in the person of Peter, is now ready to embrace fully this new direction in mission. No, it is precisely the details in the story that suggest that Luke has something else he is subtly trying to get across. So, let's play scriptural detective and see if we can tease out what Luke might be trying to tell us.

First, it is important to note where this story begins, in Joppa. Again, recognize that places matter to Luke, and this seemingly irrelevant detail is anything but. Joppa appears in a few instances in the Hebrew scriptures, but far and away its most significant use is when the reluctant prophet Jonah travelled there in order to catch a ship and sail away, all in response to a divine commission to preach to the heathen in Nineveh so that they might be saved and not destroyed. Jonah shirked his duty, ran away from his appointed task, and ran straight to Joppa to find his way onto a vessel. He later admitted why he was so reluctant, after he finally was persuaded to preach to the people of Nineveh, only to see them respond with fasting and repentance, and in turn receive a heavenly reprieve. This is precisely what Jonah had feared: "This is why I fled . . . I know that you are a merciful and compassionate God, very patient, full of faithful love, and willing not to destroy."[10] He wasn't afraid

37

that he would fail in the task given him; he was afraid that he would succeed, and that those he deemed unworthy, unclean, would somehow find grace from God. Now, Luke places Peter in that same port city of Joppa, another Jonah in a similar situation, far from eager to go and preach to those he deems unworthy, unclean. By adding the detail of Joppa, Luke has either contributed to a wild coincidence or has offered a not-so-subtle clue as to what this story is really about.

Second, it is worth noting some intriguing parallels between this story and that of Jesus and a centurion's servant in the seventh chapter of Luke's Gospel.[11] In both stories there is an emphasis on the worthiness *in Jewish terms* of the respective Gentile officer to receive what has been asked respectively of Jesus and Peter: "a God-worshipper who is well-respected by all Jewish people."[12] In this way, even as Luke records God doing a new thing, he also stresses the continuity between this new thing and its Jewish roots. Actually, Luke has offered hints about what is coming all along in his two-volume work, going all the way back to the Song of Simeon in the second chapter of his Gospel: "A light for revelation to the Gentiles / and a glory for your people Israel."[13] It is both/and, not either/or. Much more will be said about this in a subsequent chapter. What Luke seems to be saying in Cornelius's case is that nothing is lost or threatened by welcoming this outsider who has already truly proved himself!

Third, it is worth noting another parallel that Luke makes clear through Peter's comments: the Holy Spirit descends on these outsiders exactly as the Spirit earlier came to Peter and his fellow insiders in the upper room. This is another Pentecost, only the recipients of the divine empowerment are the last people the insiders would ever expect. Both Peter and his companions who are present for this moment as well as those to whom he later reports back in Jerusalem express astonishment, and then some acceptance, though later events will reveal their continued skepticism. But as Luke suggests with this Pentecost moment, if the insiders' arms are being twisted a bit to accept the inclusion of these Gentile newcomers, then it is God who is doing the arm-twisting!

Finally, it is important to note the placement of the Peter and Cornelius story immediately before the account of the Antiochene mission and Barnabas's part in it, in the second half of Acts 11. As one scholar says, what happens in Antioch is so significant that it needs to be "securely interwoven into the history of the movement's steady expansion," and confirmed by very carefully communicated apostolic approval.[14] In other words, it is as if Luke says, "Look, Peter and the others do support reaching out to the Gentiles—really!" After all, why go to all the time and trouble of presenting Peter's eventual acceptance of Gentile evangelization in the case of Cornelius, *and* immediately before the events recorded in 11:19-21, *if* Peter and the Twelve were truly enthusiastic about this mission anyway. No, it is safer to say that the story of Cornelius is included in Acts precisely to show some apostolic support for what happens next at the hands of others who are *not* the Twelve in a city that is *not* Jerusalem. It is enough for Luke that what happens next in Antioch, which is truly something new, retains some connection to Jerusalem and the apostles there, however tenuous that connection might actually be.

All of this is to say that church leaders then, like many today, might have found it easier to celebrate growth and the inclusion of newcomers as long as it all remained within comfortable, familiar terms. But when stretched beyond what is comfortable, when called to reach out to newcomers who make us nervous, it was—and still is—so much easier either to actively oppose (Paul) or passively accept (Peter) rather than proactively, intentionally, enthusiastically welcome and incorporate. Besides the fairly hostile reaction I received at that one parish I mentioned earlier, I have experienced far more occasions when my hand was shaken and a bulletin handed to me, and that is where the work of newcomer incorporation stopped, as those who might welcome me and make me feel at home were busy with one another. I always find it ironic that the vast majority of parish profiles I have ever read open with something like the following: "We are a warm and loving congregation." Perhaps it is true for those who have already made their way safely inside, but would someone still on the outside looking in agree with their description? Like Peter, it is far easier to hang out with fellow insiders in Jerusalem or Joppa than to make the time and effort to discover what God might be bringing our way through a "Cornelius" who seeks us out. It often takes folks who are still fairly new themselves, noninsiders like Barnabas of Cyprus, to show us all a more excellent way.

Radical Hospitality

What follows next in Luke's account, though often overlooked, is nothing less than extraordinary. It begins with the echo of an earlier transition statement. In Acts 8, immediately following Stephen's violent death, we were told, "At that time, the church in Jerusalem began to be subjected to vicious harassment. Everyone except the apostles was scattered throughout the regions of Judea and Samaria. . . . Those who had been scattered moved on, preaching the good news along the way."[15] Now, three chapters later, Luke both reiterates and elaborates on what he said before: "Now those who were scattered as a result of the trouble that occurred because of Stephen traveled as far as Phoenicia, Cyprus, and Antioch. They proclaimed the word only to Jews. Among them were some people from Cyprus and Cyrene. They entered Antioch and began to proclaim the good news about the Lord Jesus also to Jews who spoke Greek."[16]

With this, we are reminded of the significance of Stephen as a watershed figure in Acts. Everything changes with his martyrdom. After all, he entered the scene as part of the decision by the apostles to raise up Greek-speaking leaders to respond to Greek speakers' complaints about inequitable distribution in the previously idyllic insider community. It was suggested that the apostles' solution to the problem, while appearing effective in the short term, might in fact have simply perpetuated the status quo of parallel communities, separate from one another. We are also reminded in the transition statements of how the apostles remained in Jerusalem even as many others in the community were scattered in the aftermath of Stephen's death, taking with them the good news of God in Christ. And between these two transition statements in Acts 8 and 11, several vignettes revealed very different approaches to opening the doors to outsiders: Philip, one of the Hellenist Seven alongside Stephen, showed himself ready to share the good news with an Ethiopian outsider; Saul/Paul sought to imprison or kill any of Jesus's followers who, like Stephen, threatened to break down the boundaries between insiders and outsiders before himself being converted and called by God to be an apostle to the Gentiles; and Peter displayed first resistance and then a reluctant welcome to a God-fearing centurion.

Now, having heard the Jerusalem network proclaim with astonishment that God has given *even the Gentiles* the repentance that leads to life, Luke introduces us to this other, emerging network of believers who make their way to places like Cyprus, Phoenicia, and Antioch, some of whom proclaim the gospel *without hesitation* to outsiders as well as to Jews. Earlier, the Twelve had commissioned seven Hellenists to a specific task, to help bring about more equitable distribution and thereby silence the complaining Hellenists. Now, Luke makes a point of saying that some believers from Cyprus and Cyrene, like Barnabas, offer equal distribution—this time of the gospel message—to all whom they meet. They who were once themselves newcomers now reach out to outsiders and insiders alike, and not reluctantly but with enthusiasm. Here we see the very model of radical hospitality! As a result, the community that forms there in Antioch displays a unity in diversity that is new and unexpected, attracting the attention of Jerusalem, attracting the attention of the apostles. Their response to what they hear of this new thing is to send a representative to see firsthand what is happening. And who better to send than Barnabas?

Do notice that this is only the third time that our friend, the Levite from Cyprus, is mentioned in Acts. The first, of course, was when he showed himself to be a generous supporter of the apostolic community in Jerusalem and in turn was received with genuine affection by the Twelve. The second is when the Encourager dared to vouch for Saul/Paul when the former persecutor became a convert, standing with him before some very wary, reluctant apostles. Now, with his third appearance, Barnabas is tapped by those same apostles to check out the strange new happenings going on miles away in Antioch on the Mediterranean. Clearly, they have enough concerns that they want to make sure this new movement is in line with their own, but it is also noteworthy that they trust Barnabas enough to send him as their appointed representative. He goes, sees the good work occurring there, and rejoices! Luke further praises the Encourager by saying that he is "a good man, whom the Holy Spirit had endowed with exceptional faith."[17]

What he does next is incredible. Rather than do the work that is needed on his own, Barnabas goes down to Tarsus, finds Saul/Paul, and brings him back to be by his side. He not only vouched for Paul and introduced him to the Jerusalem leadership, but also he actually takes Paul under his wing and begins to apprentice him. Together they would meet with the believers in Antioch for a year. Intentional welcome segues into intentional training, something that will be discussed much more in the next chapter.

For now, it is enough to recognize that Barnabas is a key figure in the new thing that is taking place in Antioch. And in one of the most momentous, though oft-ignored verses in all the New Testament, we are told that it was in Antioch, not in Jerusalem, that the disciples were first called "Christians."[18] Forgive me, but this is worth repeating, just to make sure the point is clear. What could not happen in Jerusalem did happen in Antioch, for it is there that the disciples, a wonderfully mixed collection, more than a Jewish sect, became known by a new name, representing their new identity together: Christians.

Although many celebrate Pentecost each year as the birthday of the church, it is more accurate to describe it as the birth of a successful Jewish sectarian movement. And it indeed had success, but for real growth to occur, certain glass ceilings would have to be crashed through, and outsiders brought inside and truly incorporated into the community. It took persons who still remembered what it felt like to have been outside to reach out, in turn, and include others. It took a different setting, where the status quo was not yet so firmly established, where people had not yet become comfortable with the way things had always been, to allow for new possibilities. This in no way takes away all the good that had been happening in Jerusalem—it was actually quite wonderful, as Luke points out in the first several chapters of Acts—but it wasn't the goal. The risen Jesus himself had commissioned his apostles to begin in Jerusalem and then to move on, through Judea and Samaria to the ends of the earth. Now that was happening, though it was not the Twelve doing it. Luke seems to be saying that this is okay, as long as the work is indeed being done, and as long as those who are doing it are staying connected with the "mother church." It took newcomers and former outsiders to see what insiders might otherwise miss, as well as the courage and care to offer radical welcome.

The Power of Intentionality

Saul of Tarsus was afraid of seeing long-established boundaries and identity markers broken down by people like Stephen, the bold follower of Jesus who proclaimed that the temple was not needed anymore. The apostles were afraid of Saul, who professed to be a convert, but they couldn't be sure that he wasn't still a danger to them all. Peter was afraid of being contaminated by things and people he had long been taught were unclean, unworthy, unwelcome for a true, pure follower of God. The Jerusalem leaders were, if not afraid, then at least concerned, about tales coming to them about what was going on in Antioch and how it looked different from what they were used to. In the midst of all this, Barnabas returns to the stage as one who is fearless, prepared not only to vouch for Saul but also to serve as a mentor to him, ready not only to tolerate new possibilities in Antioch but also to embrace them. Fear paralyzes, but the Spirit of God empowers.

When faced with change and the breaking down of barriers between insiders and outsiders, Saul/Paul is reactive and Peter tries hard to be inactive, but Barnabas chooses to be proactive, in several ways.

First, he accepts the challenge to leave the Jerusalem community, where he and the others enjoyed past success and strong connections, and go to Antioch.

Second, he goes there with an open mind and an open heart, ready to see for himself the new thing that God might be doing which, though *not* unrecognizable, is different.

Third, he affirms the efforts of those who welcome unexpected newcomers—Hellenists as well as Hebrews—and fully incorporate them into the community.

Fourth, he chooses to stay with these faithful, fearless believers, invest his time and experience, and apprentice another in the work. Fifth, he makes sure that this new community stays connected with Jerusalem, thereby linking the emergent with the established.

For years now, I have asked congregations to consider what it would mean to "be a Barnabas," setting aside whatever fears hold them back and becoming intentional in recruiting and retaining newcomers. How do we actually do this?

First, it is essential that we let go of the persistent—and often inaccurate notion—that we are already a welcoming community, and instead test that hypothesis, inviting a "mystery shopper" to visit us and worship with us, and then report to our vestry, our leadership team, about that experience.

Second, our leadership team itself can take a "field trip" of the parish, viewing it as if through the eyes of a visitor, beginning with our website and other communications to walking through the parking lot and exploring all the church facilities, to visiting another congregation and seeing how they might do things differently.

Third, we can create a newcomer integration record, tracking our own efforts from the moment someone fills out a first-time visitor card, to making sure that the person receives a personal follow-up call from clergy and welcome letter from the vestry, to finding specific events and classes to which to invite the newcomer. Again, the goal of such a record is to help us guide the first-time visitor to fully incorporated member.

Fourth, we can make sure that our clergy and lay leaders alike receive the names of newcomers each week and add them to a personal prayer list, so that they are always thinking of them and commending them to God.

Fifth, we can explore the demographics of the area around us, becoming fully aware of the target groups around us. Are a lot of families with young children moving into the area, or is there a significant retiree population, or particular ethnic groups that might otherwise be ignored or neglected? Who are the "Hellenists" for us?

Sixth, we can consider how we might do all this not just on our own and not in a relational vacuum, but always connected with a "Jerusalem" community in a way that is mutually beneficial and supportive.

I have written elsewhere in some detail about such matters,[19] but for our purposes here let us simply appreciate that the road from Jerusalem to Antioch leads from fear to acceptance, from reactivity to intentionality, from reluctant welcome to radical hospitality. As Barnabas reminds us, growth can actually be a great adventure.

Discussion Questions

1. "Growth means headaches." What do you think of this statement that opened the chapter? Do you agree? When have you experienced this for yourself?

2. Why was it possible for things to happen in Antioch that might not have been possible in Jerusalem? What would be "Jerusalem" and "Antioch" for you, and for your church?

3. Hospitality requires an intentional decision and planning: why do you think so many congregations don't get intentional about doing it? If a report card was given to your church for new member incorporation, what grade would you give it?

4. What fears do we face in our churches and in our communities today? How do these fears affect our ways of reaching out to others?

5. Describe an example of "radical hospitality" in your own experience or that of someone you know. What did it look like? Feel like? What were the results?

Chapter 3

A Brave New World

Moving beyond Official Leadership Roles

In the beginning, Jesus called the Twelve. They were successful in fulfilling their calling, to a point. Soon thereafter he appointed the Seventy, to do what still needed to be done. Later still there came the Seven, when growth brought problems and the Twelve looked for others to handle those problems. This brings us to Antioch, to that place where the followers of Jesus became known by a new and lasting designation. Here, another group of leaders emerges, inspired by God, grounded in prayer, connected with Jerusalem, and ready to take the movement's next steps. And Barnabas is with them.

The Twelve, after their first commissioning in Luke 9, resented others who did what they themselves failed to do. Barnabas, on the other hand, actually seeks out Paul, still going by his Hebrew name Saul, in his native town of Tarsus, and brings him back to Antioch to join in the work. Barnabas doesn't have to do this. He doesn't have to get Paul. After all, Barnabas has the backing of the Twelve, who send him to Antioch when they hear of new things happening there. He clearly is well respected by all he meets there. He doesn't need Paul. But he sees something in the former persecutor that others ignored: zeal and fearlessness, yes, but perhaps also a clarity of vision that enabled Paul himself to see what others, including the Twelve, missed. Together, they join the leaders in Antioch, and then after a year are prayerfully commissioned by that same team to go and distribute the gospel message to any who will listen, Gentile as well as Jew. It is in Antioch that the disciples were first called Christians. Now, in Antioch, the Encourager and his apprentice are set apart as a new kind of "sent ones," as apostles to all.

Set Apart and Sent Out

Acts 13 opens with a description of the church leadership in Antioch, and right off the bat we see a difference from Jerusalem. Instead of the Twelve, here there are "prophets and teachers," and though they number far fewer than a dozen, they are quite a diverse group. Barnabas is mentioned first, probably confirming his important role as an emissary of the Twelve, and Saul is named last, possibly signifying his role as a leader-in-training. Besides our familiar duo, we find three others: Simeon called Niger, an intriguing designation given that *Niger* in Latin is the word for "black"; Lucius of Cyrene, whom some equate with the author Luke, though that seems doubtful; and Manean, who is described as having been brought up with the Judean ruler Herod Antipas, the son of Herod the Great who is mentioned several times in Luke's Gospel.[1] As noted, these five leaders are not designated as "apostles" like the Twelve, but rather are defined by their roles as those who communicate God's message to the community of believers. But what they do next *is* something reminiscent of Jerusalem and the Twelve, and will have far-reaching implications.

For while they are in a time of worship and fasting, the Holy Spirit tells them to "set apart" both Barnabas and Saul for the divinely appointed work. The language is quite important, as it mirrors what Jesus himself did early in Luke's Gospel when after a night of prayer he set apart the Twelve from countless unnamed disciples and then eventually sent them out as his representatives, his "sent ones."[2] Even so, now the Antiochene prophets and teachers follow the same pattern: they pray (and fast), they set apart two from among their own number, they designate them as ambassadors, and they send them out. Barnabas and Paul therefore become Antioch's own "sent ones" or apostles.

It is not terribly surprising that our dynamic duo should be the chosen ones, given that the two were already viewed as bridge-builders between this new community and the mother church, having previously been sent back to Jerusalem with funds for famine relief raised by the disciples in Antioch.[3]

This was an important mission. For if the relief funds were accepted by the leadership in Jerusalem, it could be viewed as a sign of recognition of the church in Antioch. Rejection of the gift, on the other hand, would be a devastating blow, signifying displeasure on the part of those elders with the inclusivity that marked the Antiochene community. The financial offering in this case had both practical and political dimensions, and so who better to bring it personally to the leaders in Jerusalem than the person those leaders earlier sent to Antioch, Barnabas. And so the Encourager, accompanied by his impressive apprentice, made the trip back and then later returned to Antioch from their successful humanitarian mission, bringing with them a third person, John, also known as Mark, apparently a cousin of Barnabas. Much more will be said about him later. For now, take note that the pair who had previously been sent back to Jerusalem are now being sent forward to unknown regions, this time not with funds but with the incomparable gospel of Christ.

The entire book of Acts begins to shift direction at this point, as Peter and the rest of the Jerusalem leadership, so prominent in the early part of the book, begin to fade away. Indeed, after one last appearance at the Council of Jerusalem in Acts 15, Peter and the Twelve disappear altogether. The shift begins, as so often in scripture, with a change of name for one of our protagonists. "Empowered by the Holy Spirit, Saul, also known as Paul, glared at Bar-Jesus and said . . ."[4] As mentioned already, Saul was his Hebrew name while *Paulus* or Paul was his Roman name, since his parents had somehow acquired citizenship and enabled him to be born a true child of the empire. So, as Luke notes the change from Saul to Paul, it represents a change from the person who fought so hard for the preservation of his people, Israel, to the ambassador to the Gentiles. Another subtle change occurs at this time, as "Saul and Barnabas" becomes "Paul and Barnabas," and even "Paul and his companions." The apprentice has become the leader. The one who tried desperately to silence the followers of Christ has now become a bold spokesperson. And Barnabas, the Encourager who first vouched for the convert Saul, then later sought him out and mentored him in Antioch, now allows Paul to take center stage while he himself is relegated to a supporting role. And there is still one other change.

In Acts 14:4 and again in 14:14, Paul and Barnabas are designated by the term *apostles*. Specifically, after the two have proclaimed the gospel to Gentiles as well as to Jews, after they have faced opposition on the part of Jewish leaders not unlike Paul himself in the days before his conversion, Luke says that the residents of the town of Iconium are divided, some siding with the Jewish opponents and some "with the Lord's messengers," or as other translations such as the NRSV put it, "with the apostles." This is an extraordinary thing, as the Greek term *apostoloi* (literally, "sent ones") was previously reserved for the Twelve alone. Now these new apostles, the sent ones of Antioch, the Lord's messengers, Paul and Barnabas, tell the crowd, "We are humans too, just like you! We are proclaiming the good news to you."[5] Jesus's commission on the mountain outside Jerusalem has just come a little closer to fulfillment.

Called to Be an Apostle

Let's take our leave of Acts for the moment, and turn our attention to Paul's own letters to catch a glimpse of what it meant to him to be an apostle, and why at times he displayed a certain defensiveness about his own apostleship. Consider his opening salutation to the Galatian believers: "From Paul, an apostle who is not sent from human authority or commissioned through human agency, but sent through Jesus Christ and God the Father who raised him from the dead; and from all the brothers and sisters with me. To the churches in Galatia."[6] There is nothing neutral about this greeting. To understand its intention and impact, you only have to compare it to the way he opens his first (in chronological terms) letter, written to the Thessalonian Christians: "From Paul, Silvanus, and Timothy. To the Thessalonians' church that is in God the Father and the Lord Jesus Christ."[7] Notice at once the simplicity of the salutation. There is no added self-descriptor: the writer is simply "Paul," and he writes to them alongside two of his companions, not "from all the brothers and sisters with me." This simple greeting also implies a friendly familiarity. The Thessalonians do not need to be reminded of who, or what, Paul is, for as becomes clear in the letter there is mutual respect and affection between this community and the one who brought the faith to them. Paul's salutation in his first letter, then, serves as a helpful template by which we can examine all his subsequent letters, asking why certain things might have then been added or changed, including in his very next letter, Galatians.[8]

The simplicity and familiarity of the salutation in 1 Thessalonians makes the opening in Galatians all the more jarring. From the start Paul reminds them that he is an apostle, which of course suggests that they need to be reminded. Now, for any who might question his claim, they would have had some good reason. After all, everyone knew that Jesus had personally called the Twelve to be his chosen sent ones, and even Luke's other numbered groups, the Seventy and the Seven, for all the remarkable work they did, did not claim the same status. We have seen how Peter and the others went to great length to make sure their number was restored with the casting of lots to select Matthias as the twelfth apostle, and during that selection process the point was made that he had actually accompanied Jesus for the three years of Jesus's public ministry. We can almost hear Paul's opponents in Galatia saying, "Let's face it, folks, Paul never even met Jesus! How, then, could he claim to be one of his apostles?"

How indeed? In that same salutation, Paul immediately grounds his apostleship solely on God's call, not on any selection process designed by people. No lots were cast to make him an apostle. To any who would either quietly question or openly dispute his claim to apostleship, he counters with a brief, but insightful recap of his own story. "You heard about my previous life in Judaism, how severely I harassed God's church and tried to destroy it."[9] Indeed, his reputation was well known, and he was widely feared, yet instead of trying to hide from his past or coat over it somehow, he just puts it out there and also offers a one-line explanation for why he did what he did: "I was much more militant about the traditions of my ancestors."[10] He admits that he was trying desperately to preserve what he and his fellow Jews had inherited from their forbears. He felt he had to protect the flock from dangerous wolves, even if it meant killing them.

He was admittedly an unlikely candidate for apostleship. Yet, Paul still claims he was "set apart" by God for the work from before he was even born. It is possible to hear echoes of the prophet Jeremiah, who heard the divine voice say: "Before I created you in the womb I knew you; / before you were born I set you apart; / I made you a prophet to the nations."[11] Jeremiah initially resisted his call, arguing that he was too young and inexperienced. Paul, who admits that his ambition enabled him to rise through the ranks in Judaism beyond many of his own age, appears to lack Jeremiah's modesty. But he shares the prophet's insistence that God is the one who calls and empowers. Like Jeremiah, he was set apart by God to be a prophet among "the Gentiles," a term often synonymous in scripture with "the nations." And herein lies the crux of the problem for his Galatian opponents, as becomes evident in the remainder of the letter. Like Paul himself before his conversion, they would resist any attempt at accommodation, insisting instead on circumcision for Gentile converts, thereby returning to the notion of the church as a Jewish messianic sect.

Much more will be said about all this in chapter 5, especially given the horrendous consequences it has on Barnabas and Paul's relationship. For now, it is important to note that although Paul's opponents' issue with him concerned Gentile inclusion, the manner in which they chose to go after him was to challenge his apostleship. In his letter he responds with confidence that it is God who commissioned him, and this is why he did not immediately confer with "the men who were apostles before me."[12] And when he did finally make it to Jerusalem, Paul again seems to boast that he did not see any of the apostles except Peter—intriguingly referred to here by the Aramaic form of his name, Cephas—and James the Just, brother of Jesus and eventually de facto leader of the Jerusalem community, though interestingly not even a member of the Twelve. In marked contrast to the Thessalonian correspondence, the letter to the Galatians clearly shows Paul's apostleship under fire. And it doesn't end there!

As with Galatians, the next two letters Paul wrote, 1 and 2 Corinthians, likewise open with Paul speaking of himself as an apostle. And, again, it soon becomes evident in these letters that he is writing to a community in which some have questioned his status and become susceptible to whatever propaganda his enemies would use against him. Indeed, in Corinth there appears to be not one group of opponents against him, but rather multiple factions at work against each other, each one claiming a patron, as it were: Cephas (again, Paul uses Peter's Aramaic name), Apollos (not one of the Twelve, but a charismatic and popular evangelist), and Paul himself. There is even a fourth group that speaks of belonging to Christ, as if the other groups do not also ultimately belong to Christ. Aware that his one letter will be read by all the competing groups, Paul boldly states that he was called by God to be an apostle and, even more, that he "gave birth to you in Christ Jesus through the gospel."[13] As the Corinthian Christians' father, the *paterfamilias* of that extended family, Paul is ready to take on all those "arrogant people" who would dare to challenge him. As he later asks, "Am I not free? Am I not an apostle? Haven't I seen Jesus our Lord? Aren't you my work in the Lord? If I'm not an apostle to others, at least I am to you! You are the seal that shows I'm an apostle. This is my defense against those who criticize me."[14] In the argument he then makes about his right to be counted among "the rest of the apostles, the Lord's brothers, and Cephas,"[15] he includes Barnabas right there alongside himself. Even more than in Galatians, he points to the strong familial relationship he has with the Corinthians, his beloved children in the Lord.

It appears that his first letter to the Corinthians does little good in eliminating the problems, for in 2 Corinthians we see even more vigorous opposition against him from a group he classifies as "false apostles" and "dishonest workers."[16] These appear to be much more like those opponents he faced in Galatia, as they go after him personally, contrasting him with the established leadership. Twice, Paul counters with the bold claim that "I don't consider myself as second-rate in any way compared to the 'super-apostles,'"[17] and if he boasts, it is not in credentials—though he is quick to remind the Corinthians of his impressive Jewish and Christian credentials—but rather in the authority and the power of God, which shines through his own weakness and by which Paul has been able to build up and tear down the congregation there.

Finally, Paul's letter to the Romans also opens with the claim that he is an apostle, "set apart for God's good news."[18] Here, the issue is not a group of opponents coming in after Paul has founded the community and trying to turn its members against him. Rather, the Christian community in Rome came into existence apart from Paul, and he is personally unknown to them, although clearly they have heard much about him. And so, having previously "been stopped so many times from coming to see you,"[19] he now is making preparations to arrive, and therefore sets out the longest and most detailed exposition of his faith, focusing once again on the issue of unity that we find in Christ, whether Jew or Gentile. In introducing himself to the community there, he does not need to defend his apostleship as with the Galatians and Corinthians, but simply claims it as a self-description. He is their servant, but he is also a divinely appointed apostle. Indeed, as in those other more contentious situations, Paul's self-proclaimed status as one of Jesus's "sent ones" is grounded not in the approval of the Jerusalem hierarchy, but in God.

Pride or Something Else?

So what does all this talk about apostleship mean for us? I mean, today we speak of priests, pastors, and preachers; wardens, vestry, and elders; but we don't usually speak of apostles. And why should we care about Paul's position anyway? At the heart of so many criticisms of Paul is this idea that he was full of himself, arrogant, egocentric, someone who didn't listen to anyone else. Perhaps some think that all this talk of defending his apostleship just sounds high and mighty on Paul's part, one more way that he picks a fight with others, one more reason not to like him. But they would be wrong!

If we consider Paul's own letters, all his talk about apostleship was not simply to feed his own ego. As he himself says more than once, if he was seeking human approval, he never would have chosen to be a follower of Christ. No, his ongoing attempts to defend his apostleship were not as much about ego as about being taken seriously in the task of reaching out to the Gentiles as God's chosen ambassador and including them in the household of God. It is like those who work hard to earn a degree, not so they can brag about having letters after their names, but so others might take into account the years of research and work that have gone into what they are saying or writing. We must take our work, the mission to which we are called, quite seriously, but we can never take ourselves too seriously. Paul would agree.

Apostleship was crucial to Paul, therefore, not because he wanted people to see how great or impressive he was, but because recognition of his apostleship would carry an implicit acknowledgment of the divine imprimatur on that radical mission and message. In the chapters that follow, we will explore just how dangerous Paul was to those who sought to believe in Christ while maintaining accepted societal boundaries and patterns. For now, we should note that his claim of apostleship actually served to support all those underdogs who found a home in the churches that he founded, all those who once were far off but now had been brought near to God and to one another, whatever their status outside the community of believers. Opponents and saboteurs constantly tried to derail his work of inclusion, and one of their chief weapons was the Twelve's obvious pedigree as those who had been with Jesus for three years. Paul, for his part, kept coming back to the fact that the risen Christ had appeared to him as well, even if he was "born at the wrong time." In response to those who said that he was not on par with the Twelve, he did not disagree—"I'm the least important of the apostles. I don't deserve to be called an apostle, because I harassed God's church"—but he asserted that ultimately "I am what I am by God's grace," not to mention the fact that because of the disadvantages, he "worked harder than all the others."[20] For Paul, the only approval, the only backing that really mattered was God's, and that was more than enough, not just for him as an apostle, but for all the underdogs in the Christian community who could otherwise be seen as second class. "If God is for us," Paul would remind them in Romans, "who is against us?"[21]

One Body, Different Gifts

Having defended his authority, then, this apostle set out to articulate a different paradigm for the Christian community and how it can function. Perhaps because Barnabas had once seen in him what the Twelve and others missed, perhaps because Barnabas and he together had been part of a diverse team of prophets and teachers in Antioch—whatever the source of his thinking, in 1 Corinthians Paul speaks of the community as akin to the human body. "Christ is just like the human body—a body is a unit and has many parts; and all the parts of the body are one body, even though there are many."[22] In the body, Paul asserts, no one part can dismiss the importance of another. "The eye can't say to the hand, 'I don't need you.'"[23] In this body, all are welcome; all have a part to play; all are to be honored. What Paul offers here is nothing less than a manifesto of individual value and interdependence for the Christian community.

It is important to note the context of these familiar words. Paul's exposition on the body comes toward the end of a letter that addresses so many issues of arrogance, not on his part but on the part of those who thought

55

themselves better than others in the community because they looked to a particular leader, whether Peter, Apollos, or Paul himself or because they had more money and could afford to sue fellow members in court or because they held more impressive positions in the surrounding culture or because they could speak in tongues or were known for their spirituality. The list goes on and on, and Paul tackles each issue head-on throughout the letter. But it culminates in his body imagery and the interdependence represented therein. Though he could have acted arrogantly and set up his own breakaway movement—after all, one of the sectarian subgroups in Corinth lifted him up as their inspiration—Paul chooses instead to remind the entire diverse group that they all need one another, that they suffer and rejoice together.

Within this interdependent body, he explains that they all have distinctive roles to play and lists them in order: apostles, prophets, teachers; deeds of power, gifts of healing, forms of assistance, forms of leadership, various kinds of tongues. All are important. All are needed. But the order is not arbitrary. In Antioch, Paul and Barnabas were included among a group of prophets and teachers. But having been sent out from Antioch to spread the good news and plant churches, to Corinth and those other places where he successfully established Christians communities, Paul is an apostle. There is both humility and hierarchy in this body analogy. Christ is the head, not Paul or Peter or anyone else. But in the ordering of their common life, Paul claims some precedence even as he lifts up the value of the otherwise voiceless underdogs.

Then, this same leader whom so many have since accused of being arrogant, boastful, and conceited, presents one of the most beautiful, one of the most poignant descriptions ever written of the thread that binds the body together. "If I speak in tongues of human beings and of angels but I don't have love, I'm a clanging gong or a clashing cymbal."[24] How fascinating that this passage is read most often in the context of weddings, with people nodding and smiling at the couple as they hear these words. Yet Paul is not writing this in the context of romantic love between two people, but rather as a very practical antidote to the arrogance that infects a community, undermines authority, and creates divisions. Consider the list of attributes he offers. "Love is patient, love is kind, it isn't jealous, it doesn't brag, it isn't arrogant, it isn't rude, it doesn't seek its own advantage, it isn't irritable, it doesn't keep a record of complaints, it isn't happy with injustice, but it is happy with the truth. Love puts up with all things, trusts in all things, hopes for all things, endures all things."[25] These aren't just pretty words; they are powerful challenges.

Many times have I called on Paul's words here to challenge congregational leaders. If they—no, if you—were to write up a report card based on these attributes of love, what kind of grades would be marked? Imagine simply replacing the word *love* with the pronoun *I* or, in thinking about the congregation as a whole or its leadership, *we*. Then read the litany of attributes once more, this time as questions: "Am I patient? Am I kind? Or am I in any way envious, boastful, arrogant, or rude?" Or this becomes a statement of intentionality for our leadership: "We together will not insist on our own way. We together will indeed bear and believe and hope and endure all things." If only the church in Corinth had really listened to Paul and taken these challenges seriously. If only we as individuals and churches would dare to do so today!

So, back to an earlier question: why should we care that Paul was an apostle? And why should we take him seriously? The answer is quite simple: he is offering us a vital and life-giving way to exist together in Christian community. Who cares, Paul says, who our leader is? Who cares if we are impressive for some reason? The issue, the real issue, is to see how we treat one another for, as the old folk song says, they will know we are Christians by our love. It is certainly easier to love one another when we are so much like one another, similar in background, status, and opinion. But when we are Jews *and* Greeks, when we are slaves *and* free, when we have different gifts and perform different roles, then things get much more complicated, and it is harder to be a loving, grace-filled body.

But Paul knew from personal experience that this is possible. Indeed, you might say he learned from the best. After all, no one in Jerusalem wanted anything to do with him when he first came on the scene—no one, that is, except Barnabas. And the Encourager showed him what a community grounded in extraordinary respect and concern could be when he took him under his wing to Antioch. As Saul the Pharisee, the persecutor of followers of Jesus, he already knew how to resist and confront. As Paul the apprentice, he learned how to include others and nurture them in the use of their unique gifts. And this, Paul asserts, is all part of being an apostle.

Nurturing Leaders in Our Congregations

In a visit to a particular parish, the priest told me that they had made huge strides in greeting newcomers and helping them feel welcome. But the problem was that they could not seem to retain them; after a fairly long honeymoon period, the newcomers would quietly slip away. Throwing up his hands, he asked, "What can we do?" This is a very familiar tale, one that I have heard or witnessed countless times. The solution is actually quite simple, though not necessarily easy. It involves changing how things are run in a congregation or, more specifically, who is running things. As long as we work under the 20/80 principle, in which 20 percent of the members are doing 80 percent of the work, then we are unable to tap into, or even see, the treasures that God brings to us with each new arrival. As long as we see newcomers simply as potential pledge units to help shore up the existing budget and support existing programs, then change is not possible. And sooner or later these persons will figure this out. A few will stay on and become loyal supporters of the status quo, always slightly disconnected, unable to share the laughter over inside jokes and stories about the good old days. Of course, many more will simply find their way quietly to the door.

Barnabas could have taken either option. He did, after all, come on the stage with his checkbook out, ready to support the programs and pastoral needs of the Jerusalem community. And, because he was generous and encouraging, he was welcomed warmly by that community. He might have stayed on forever in that group, there in the shadow of the temple, or he might later have become frustrated and simply left. But when the Twelve sent him as their representative to Antioch, he found something truly exciting, a group that not only welcomed newcomers but also proactively sought them out and not just those who looked and talked like the existing members but entirely different folks altogether. Barnabas clearly understood the importance of nurturing fresh leadership, for he sought out Paul and took him back to Antioch to join him in the work. It was not long before others in that community recognized both Barnabas's and Paul's gifts, for they were soon part of the leadership team, then sent further out as Antioch's own "sent ones."

I shared all this with that priest and the lay leaders of the parish, and they took notice of how the Antioch story contrasted with their own experience. Newer members were incorporated into every level of the church's life in Antioch, even the senior leadership team. As these individuals reminded me, all too often, we see the same names put forward for vestries and key committees, simply because they are familiar to us. We know they will accept, and we know they will get the jobs done. And while it is helpful to have both experience and institutional memory represented on our leadership teams, it is also helpful—no, it is crucial—to have some fresh insights and different thoughts. The priest and lay leaders with whom I was speaking nodded their heads, understanding how far they were from Antioch. So, together we envisioned what could be done to "be a Barnabas" and move forward into a brave new world of intentional leadership development.

First, recognize the importance of apprenticeship. Barnabas looked at the good work already being done in Antioch and immediately saw an opportunity to train Saul of Tarsus and help him grow in the use of his gifts in the midst of a healthy system. Too often we fall into one of two traps, either burning out new staff or volunteers by throwing too much at them too fast, or failing to tap them on the shoulder in the first place and relying only on ourselves and on those who have always done the work. We need to find the Pauls in our congregation, and if they are a bit rough around the edges, then we can work with them to hone their skills and discern their place in the system.

Second, welcome the benefits of a leadership team. We do not have to bear the burdens of leadership on our own. Despite the image of Paul as a lone wolf that some have projected onto him, in his letters he always mentions his colleagues in ministry and gives thanks to God for them. Again and again he speaks of the importance of sharing the work. And in the story of Antioch's leadership team in Acts, we see the fruits of their teamwork and a model for our own congregations. Too many churches today are pastor-centric and too many pastors or priests end up feeling overwhelmed and underappreciated. This pattern gets replayed throughout the parish, as eager volunteers end up getting major tasks put on their shoulders and follow the pastor in feeling overwhelmed and underappreciated. And so it goes on and on. A healthy leadership team can model for the entire congregation the benefits of sharing the ministry.

Third, establish all leadership development in prayer. This may sound obvious, but it is so much easier in church life to work, work, and work harder, than to stop for a moment, be still, and know that God is God. Prayer is about listening, not just speaking. It is about seeking to discern the Spirit's voice, and that takes some stillness. The leaders in Antioch understood this, and it was only after a period of prayer and fasting that they sent out Barnabas and Paul as their apostles, their missionaries. We today are blessed with beautiful liturgies, and can with some creativity and intentionality find ways to commission leaders for many tasks, both within the life of the congregation and for the world around us. We can also call for prayer vigils before seeking and electing leaders such as on the vestry. And our vestry members, our leadership team, should consider as part of their responsibilities daily prayer for our fellow parishioners, for newcomers, for our surrounding community, for different parts of our larger church and Communion.

The priest I visited realized that greeting a first-time visitor is only the beginning of a process in which some will eventually outshine us, as Barnabas learned firsthand with Paul. But for now, we must stop, take a breath, and remember that God is God, and then look around us to see who God has brought into our lives to support and disciple. Paul knew that he was someone whom Barnabas dared to trust when others refused to do so. Barnabas trusted him, vouched for him, took him under his wing, and helped him find his way forward as a witness of Christ to Gentiles and Jews alike. To be a Barnabas today means searching for our Pauls, our Phoebes, Timothys, and Lydias, and then assisting them in their own development in Christ. Paul defended his apostleship so vigorously because a lot of people depended on him, the first-century underdogs—women, slaves, Gentiles—and because he remembered what it was like to be dismissed. Apostleship for Paul was not about arrogance. It was about being taken seriously. For like the one who encouraged him, Paul was determined to nurture a new generation of apostles, prophets, teachers, and evangelists, to help members of the body of Christ discern the gifts they had to offer and the important role that they could play.

Discussion Questions

1. What do you think about the church in Antioch commissioning its own set of "sent ones"? Should they have consulted instead with the Twelve, and perhaps had Jerusalem send out a delegation on their behalf?

2. The word *apostle* was previously reserved for the Twelve alone. What does the term *apostle* mean to you? What are the essential requirements for apostleship?

3. Paul spent considerable energy defending his apostleship. Was it worth the effort? What do you think of his defense? Would you have been convinced by his arguments? Are you convinced now?

4. Earlier I said that in this body, all are welcome and all have a part to play. How true is this for your own congregation? Are there ways in which people are welcomed as newcomers, but not fully incorporated in the life and leadership of the congregation?

5. Who are you apprenticing? What is your leadership team's plan for helping all members of the congregation to discern their gifts and live into their ministry?

Chapter 4

To Honor or Accommodate

Moving beyond Jewish Roots

Bowing slightly, he presents me with his business card, clasping it between the thumbs and forefingers of both hands with the print facing me. Offering a small bow in return, I receive the card in similar fashion, using both hands, and raising it just enough to read it slowly and with deliberation. I then look up and, nodding, utter a quiet "Xie xie," or "Thank you," before placing the card with great care in the pocket of my suit jacket. I then repeat the same with the presentation of my card to my Shanghai colleague.

It is such a small thing in the grand scheme of life: the exchange of business cards. Yet, perhaps without us even realizing it, this small thing actually can be an opportunity to honor—or offend. Most of us are familiar with the old adage, "It's the little things that count," but at no time is this more accurate than when we are engaged in any kind of intercultural communication. Our body language, our tone, our choice of words and idioms—all play a vital part in our interactions, and all can become tools of shared meaning or unintentional weapons of discord, depending on how they are utilized. And before we assume that this is simply about international relations, let me say that I am reminded every time I spend time with my kids and their friends that I am in terra incognita. That culture has its own language, its own rituals, its own experiences, and I am most certainly an outsider looking in.

The old Saul of Tarsus dreaded the thought that the centuries-old boundaries that had both defined and protected his Jewish people from being swallowed up by one heathen superpower after another were somehow being broken down by the followers of Jesus. Some of those followers, like Peter and John, went out of their way to prop up the boundaries and strengthen their Jewish connectedness. But troublemakers like Stephen pointed toward the possibilities that Saul, the Pharisee from Tarsus, so desperately feared. Later, as Paul, the apostle from Antioch, along with his mentor and partner Barnabas, not only let go of those earlier fears but also became committed to breaking down those same boundaries and incorporating others into a new extended family. To do this, new language, new rituals, new shared experiences were needed. He and Barnabas were ready to supply them.

And, as expected, there were others who were just as ready to resist.

Apostles to the Gentiles

How appropriate that the first destination for the newly appointed "sent ones" from Antioch was Cyprus, the island home of Joseph the Levite, also known as Barnabas. He and Saul, along with Barnabas's cousin John Mark—but more about him next chapter—made their way to Salamis, the bustling seaport on the eastern shore of the island that according to legend had been founded by Teucer the archer following the Trojan War. In that legend, Teucer was later exiled from Salamis by his own father, but not before uttering words that might well have crossed the minds of the arriving Barnabas and Saul: "Do not despair, for tomorrow we shall set out upon the vast ocean."[1] Certainly, a great journey lay before this duo! But it all started there in Barnabas's old familiar territory. There they began their preaching crusade in the city's synagogues, before making their way some ninety miles straight across the width of the island. And it is there that we glimpse a soon-to-be recognizable pattern.

Barnabas and Saul visit a synagogue. They find a small group intrigued but the majority unwilling to respond. They turn to Gentiles with their message. The outsiders respond with enthusiasm. The synagogue majority reacts with opposition or violence. Upon reflection, it is a pattern that seems to be in direct contrast to what we saw with Peter and the Twelve in the opening chapters of Acts. There they preached and healed and shared communion, and still remained faithful to the daily temple worship. Opposition did come their way, but only when they came too close to breaking down boundaries, as when they cured a lame man on the Sabbath like Jesus before them. But following each of their arrests and questioning, Peter and the others went right back to the temple and continued to live their dual lives. For Barnabas, and especially for Saul, such a pattern soon became impossible to maintain.

But this does not happen all at once, and for a while, the duo tries to straddle the tightrope without ending up dead . . . sometimes literally. Consider their initial forays. First of all, there is the encounter with Sergius Paulus, the proconsul of Cyprus, "an intelligent man"[2] as Luke describes him, who comes to faith as a result of hearing them. How wonderful, how utterly appropriate, that this first convert was a Roman proconsul, a Gentile and not a Jew. And how awful that the person who tried to stand between Sergius Paulus and the two apostles was a Jewish magician and false prophet, Elymas bar-Jesus. Notice also that a change takes place with this story, as "Barnabas and Saul" becomes "Paul and Barnabas." It occurs subtly, as an aside, as the proconsul asks to hear their message and "Saul, also known as Paul"[3] begins to speak. Some say that the transition to his Roman name was in honor of this first convert. Whatever the reason, Saul is no more, and Paul has found his voice. And he quickly shows that he is ready to use it.

Paul and Barnabas depart Cyprus and sail to Turkey, stopping off in Perga, about twelve miles inland, where John Mark leaves their company. Though many have speculated on the reasons for his departure—health problems, fear about the difficulties they would face on the upcoming journey, disagreement with Paul's commitment to accepting Gentiles in without having them accept the requirements of the Jewish law—Acts remains silent on the specifics. Whatever the reason for John Mark's exit, it proves to be a sore point for Paul, and leads to the eventual end of his partnership with Barnabas, something to be explored in the next chapter. For now, we see that the pair press on and traverse the Taurus mountains northward one hundred miles to the city of Antioch Pisidia. This is, of course, one of the dozen or more Antiochs that came into being around the year 300 BCE as a way for the ruler Seleucus Nikator to honor his father Antiochus. As the sent ones from Syrian Antioch made their way into Pisidian Antioch, they were entering the leading city of the southern part of the Roman province of Galatia, a "colony city" with the privileges of local autonomy and tax-exempt status within the empire. They also were entering a city with a large Jewish community and again found the local synagogue in which to begin their work.

There, as reported in Acts 13, following "the reading of the Law and the Prophets," Paul and Barnabas are encouraged to offer a "a sermon."[4] The primary audience is "fellow Israelites and Gentile God-worshippers," meaning this is a message from one insider in the Jewish system to fellow insiders.[5] What follows, much like the earlier sermons in Acts by Peter and Stephen, is an exposition of the Hebrew scriptures beginning with the exodus and moving quickly through God's call to King David, "a man who shares [God's] desires," then fast-forwarding to David's descendant, Jesus, the promised savior of Israel who was killed only to be resurrected through the power of God.[6] Most of the message is fairly innocuous, an interesting midrash on the scriptures, but Paul begins to move into more sensitive territory in his conclusion that "From all those sins from which you couldn't be put in right relationship with God through Moses' Law, through Jesus everyone who believes is put in right relationship with God."[7] Still, even with this suggestion that Jesus could do what the blessed Torah could not, many in the audience wanted to hear more. But the following week, when a much larger crowd showed up, some jealous religious leaders fought back, resulting in Paul and Barnabas reacting with words that would signal a radical change that will have profound implications: "We had to speak God's word to you first. Since you reject it and show that you are unworthy to receive eternal life, we will turn to the Gentiles."[8] The move to the Gentiles is backed by a citation from Isaiah 49:6, a key verse in Luke's Gospel and Acts, about the chosen one being "as light to the nations / so that my salvation may reach to the end of the earth."

And so begins that pattern of preaching to the insiders, with acceptance by some and resistance by far more, followed by a move to the outsiders that in turn provokes violent reaction from the insiders. It occurs in Iconium, an ancient city on a plateau over three thousand feet in elevation, located about ninety miles southeast of Antioch on the route connecting Ephesus with Syria. Like Paul and Barnabas's previous destinations, Iconium was a demographically diverse city. So too are the duo's next destinations, the Galatian towns of Derbe and Lystra, smaller in size yet containing a Roman military outpost. The pattern continues: some insiders respond positively, more react violently, and outsiders rejoice. In the midst of all this, we see Luke use the term *apostles*, which is usually reserved for the Twelve, but here applied to Paul and Barnabas, God's ambassadors to the Gentiles.

Different People, Different Messaging

The dilemma these two "sent ones" face is how to honor their heritage while accommodating newcomers who don't share that heritage and for whom that heritage can actually get in the way of incorporation. Earlier in Acts, we saw how it was precisely when the church was growing and newcomers joining in great numbers that problems began to merge. And that was with Hellenists, non-Palestinian Jewish followers of Christ. Now, the people hearing Paul and Barnabas are actually non-Jews. Predictably, new problems emerge. "The gods have come down to us in human form!" So shout the Lycaonians, believing Barnabas to be Zeus and Paul, Hermes, "because he was the chief speaker."[9] It is not what the two were expecting. This kind of acclamation would not help.

As to why the Lycaonians mistake our intrepid duo for Greek gods, the answer might lie in the Roman poet Ovid, whose famous *Metamorphoses* recounts a tale of two strangers who visit a town seeking welcome and hospitality, only to be rejected by all but one elderly couple.[10] The strangers are revealed to be Zeus and Hermes. Much like the wicked masses in the story of Noah, the townspeople who rejected the visitors in turn face the terror of a great flood. As for the couple who opened their home to the disguised gods, their small home is beautifully transformed into a gilded temple. Is it any surprise that the people of Lystra take no chances when Paul and Barnabas come into their midst, with bold words and miraculous deeds? The problem, of course, is that Paul and Barnabas are not looking to be revered or deified. Far from it! They seek ultimately to get out of the way and let Christ become real to all those they encounter. This is why they tear the clothes in a supreme gesture of sorrow over the actions of their worshippers, begging them to cease this useless activity and turn instead to the living God.

What is interesting is how Paul and Barnabas communicate their message. We begin to see a difference in the language and imagery used in the preaching. Paul's message in the synagogue at Antioch Pisidia was virtually the same as Peter's at Pentecost, drawing on citations from the Hebrew scriptures that would have been understood and appreciated by Jewish listeners. But here was a very different group, and the old familiar words would be completely lost on this audience. And so the apostles to the Gentiles speak in a way that the Gentiles can understand and appreciate. They speak of the difference between visible idols and the unseen Creator. They draw on the natural world to show the kindness of God, who gives "rain from above as well as seasonal harvests, and satisfying you with food and happiness."[11]

This new messaging is even more evident later on, when Paul addresses a group of Athenians in the famous Mars Hill sermon of Acts 17. Designated as such for the hill northwest of the Acropolis in Athens named for Mars, the Roman version of the Greek god of war, Ares, the site was also referred to as the Areopagus. While waiting for his colleagues to meet up with him, Paul found himself furious by what he saw. Though no longer the financial or political hub that it had been in earlier days, Athens remained a cultural mecca, with artists and students, not to mention countless tourists, all enjoying its great art and architecture. The most impressive of the buildings were often temples dedicated to one deity or another, so that it is little surprise that Paul would find it to be a "city of idols."[12]

There he encounters Epicureans and Stoics, who want to hear a word from him. The Epicureans and Stoics were interesting groups, quite different from each other. The first group was focused on the material side of life and had little use for discussion of gods and goddesses. The second group were pantheists and believed that the divine was to be found in all human beings, exemplified above all in reason. As we see in Luke's tale, representatives of the two groups approach Paul, taunting him a bit as a dilettante or babbler, literally a "seed-speaker" or one who sows ideas here and there without much thought. He goes on to show them just how focused and strategic he really is. These are not Jews, nor even monotheists. They hear him speak of Jesus and figure this must be a new god who could be added to their ever-expanding pantheon. Instead Paul meets them where they are, affirming them as being very "religious" in light of the number of temples and altars they have. He even notes the altar he saw to an *unknown* god. "What you worship as unknown, I now proclaim to you."[13] Now, with a play on the very words he once heard Stephen utter, Paul proclaims that God does not live "in temples made with human hands. Nor is God served by human hands, as though he needed something." Rather, he says, God "gives life, breath, and everything else."[14]

Most remarkable is what follows, as Paul moves from the living witness to the Creator God in the natural world to the Athenians' own poets. Lacking sacred scriptures like the Torah and Prophets that Paul had studied all his life, the most memorable written texts for these Greeks would have been their poets, playwrights, and philosophers. Paul quotes from two of them when he professes that "In God we live, move, and exist," and again, "we are his offspring."[15] He uses these to point out the absurdity of thinking that idols made by human hands can be living deities. But again, it is important to take note that instead of using the Hebrew scriptures, which would have accomplished little or nothing, or even had a backfiring effect, Paul instead shows flexibility by using the language, the imagery, and the writings that are important to this different audience.

Somewhat surprisingly, Luke does not report great success in response to the sermon, listing as converts only one man, one woman, and some unnamed others. Paul does not stay in Athens, in fact, but instead moves on to Corinth, where he finds new partners like Priscilla and her husband Aquila (much more will be said about Priscilla later in chapter 6). There he spends an extended period of time, much like Antioch, and a church community is born and develops, one with more Gentiles than Jews. Later still, in his first letter to the Corinthian Christians, Paul urges those believers to be mindful of the outsider, to beware of speaking in indiscernible tongues unless there is someone present to interpret what is being said. It is a warning fit for all ages and peoples, for it is all about the danger of insider language and how it can create barriers between "us" and "them." As Paul puts it, "If you praise God in the Spirit, how will the people who aren't trained in that language say 'Amen!' to your thanksgiving, when they don't know what you are saying?"[16] Now, while the situation being addressed in 1 Corinthians concerns some kind of glossolalia or ecstatic tongues, the fact remains that anytime "insider speak" is used, newcomers, especially those coming from a very different background, are excluded.

But all this is down the road for Paul. Returning to Acts 14, we see him with Barnabas, already conscious of the importance of language and messaging, intentionally doing what needs to be done to interpret the good news that might otherwise be indecipherable to non-Jews. With great care, aware of the fragility of the systems that have recently been birthed, the two retrace their steps and in each place encourage the church leaders who will carry on the work they have initiated. In all this, Paul and Barnabas, apostles to the Gentiles, have begun to build intercultural bridges that will turn the world upside down and lead to an inevitable confrontation.

The Council

Now, despite the title of this book, so far the situation has not been Barnabas *versus* Paul, but rather Barnabas and Paul versus everyone else, or at least versus a lot of people who thought *just like Paul himself used to think.* The issue was one of boundaries. There are Jews and there are Gentiles, and the walls that separate are there to protect the Jews from being either wiped out or swallowed whole. As Paul himself knew, the dangers were real. The Twelve knew this too, and did all they could to honor their heritage and not send danger signals to the Jewish leadership in Jerusalem. And for many others among the Jewish followers of Jesus, while open to the occasional Gentile coming into the fold, they believed that there already existed a means to do this and still honor the age-old boundaries. There was a clear procedure by which the convert could visibly show the seriousness of taking on the responsibilities of following the Torah. That way, that procedure, was circumcision.

For adult male converts to Judaism, circumcision was understood to be the clearest, most direct way of crossing over from the pagan world into the world of God's chosen people. For some of the Jewish Christians in Jerusalem and Judea, it was no different for Gentile converts to Christianity. Inasmuch as Jesus was understood to be the Jewish Messiah, the hope of Israel, then it only made sense to these Judaizers, as Paul would call them, to make circumcision a requirement for outsiders wanting to come in. Some of these come to Antioch to "correct" this neglected point in Barnabas and Paul's teaching. The missionary pair, of course, "took sides against these Judeans and argued strongly against their position."[17] So in the midpoint in Luke's narrative, the lines are drawn and the battle for the future of the faith takes place.

Note that Paul and Barnabas's decision to go to Jerusalem is not theirs alone. Rather, they are "appointed" by the leaders in Antioch, even as they had been set apart and sent off on their earlier apostolic journey. And this time, others are chosen to accompany them on the 250-mile journey to Jerusalem, possibly including a young man named Titus who will go on to become a regular companion of Paul's.[18]

Of course, some might ask why they would need to go to Jerusalem at all. Why not deal with the issue there in Antioch? The answer may lie partly in the fact that the antagonists are not from Antioch, but come instead from the region of Judea. It is likely that believers back in Jerusalem had been hearing multiple complaints from Jewish Christians and/or non-Christian Jews about the disturbances that seemed to follow Barnabas and Paul wherever they went. Barnabas and Paul could claim great successes in conversions, no doubt, but they also had made a lot of enemies. Word likely would have reached Jerusalem and Judea, and some might have decided that the potential cost was too high and made their way to Antioch to deal with the duo.

The other reason, perhaps the more significant one, for Paul and Barnabas and some others to go to Jerusalem was recognition of the ongoing connection with the "mother church" and its leadership. The apostles of Antioch knew that their work on behalf of the Gentiles would be largely for naught if the "apostles and elders" in Jerusalem refused to recognize those efforts and perhaps even cut them off. A solely internal judgment would be inadequate in this crucial case, for too much was riding on it. For the Christian mission to move forward, to grow and flourish, it was important for Barnabas and Paul to retain their roots in the original Jesus movement in Jerusalem. For this reason above all, they made the journey to plead their case to those who preceded them.

The journey itself is full of celebration, as Paul and Barnabas literally reverse the path originally set by Jesus in his apostolic commission, going back through Samaria and Judea to Jerusalem itself, and sharing with all the disciples in each place their stories of God's work among the Gentiles. But their opponents are ready. There, before the apostles and elders, these believers "from among the Pharisees" declare that "the Gentiles must be circumcised. They must be required to keep the Law from Moses."[19] While they contend that this is for the converts' sake, for "unless you are circumcised according to the custom we've received from Moses, you can't be saved,"[20] it may be argued both by their vehemence and by the eventual solution they accept that the real concern of these Pharisees is about how they would be affected by unregulated Gentile inclusion.

Looking back two thousand years, it should be noted that the issue, of course, was never about what we would call the moral law, as exemplified in the Ten Commandments and other ethical precepts. After all, most of the major world religions contain something like the Decalogue or the Golden Rule. Rather, the controversy regarded what is referred to as the ritual law, those purity rules and regulations that helped define members of the group. Food laws, intermarriage prohibitions, worship regulations—they all had the effect of keeping insiders insulated and protected from the ever-encroaching outside world. This way of thinking is what earlier prompted Saul of Tarsus to do everything in his power to fight against members of the Way altogether. Unlike Saul, these opponents of full Gentile inclusion were indeed followers of Christ, but we might well say that they were somehow more *Christian Jews* than they were *Jewish Christians*. It was fine for the Gentiles to believe in Jesus, but unless they became Jews, they could not eat with them.

For one last time in Acts, Peter takes center stage as he stands and speaks to the Council assembly. Sharing once more the familiar (to us) tale of his encounter with Cornelius and his household, Peter reminds them all that God gave the Holy Spirit to the Gentiles just as God once gave the Spirit to the Apostles and other believers in the upper room in Jerusalem. "He made no distinction between us and them, but purified their deepest thoughts and desires through faith."[21] Peter goes on to argue that demanding circumcision of these Gentile converts, far from helping them, would be "placing a burden on the shoulders of these disciples that neither we not our ancestors could bear."[22] It was a bold statement, but as we will see next chapter, for Peter old habits die hard. For now, it is good to see that Paul and Barnabas are not alone, and that "the Rock" in this crucial moment stands with them as they begin to share their stories of God's work among the Gentiles.

The next to speak, and indeed the council's convener and final arbiter, is James, the brother of Jesus. Now, there are several persons named James in the New Testament, including the son of Zebedee who with his brother John and Simon Peter was one of the inner circle who accompany Jesus at key moments in his ministry.[23] There is also James the son of Alphaeus, another member of the Twelve,[24] as well as James "the Less."[25] And there is James, the father of the other apostle Judas, not Iscariot. It can become confusing! And then there is the James with whom we are concerned here, the brother of Jesus, who in the Gospels is mentioned by name only twice, along with three other brothers (as well as unnamed sisters).[26] Named first both times, he might have been the eldest, after Jesus. None of the brothers seems to have believed in Jesus until after his resurrection, but then they are present at Pentecost, and James soon rises to prominence.[27] His nickname, "the Just," may well be the result of his concern for honoring the Jewish law.

In any case, it is noteworthy that Peter and the apostles seem to be fading from view as James and the elders rise to roles of leadership in the Jerusalem church. It is James who hears Peter speak, then Paul and Barnabas, and finally adds his authoritative decision. Affirming Peter's testimony (referring to him by a variation of his Aramaic name Simeon or Simon), James goes on to support the Gentile position by drawing on the scriptures, especially the prophet Amos, which speak of the Gentiles as God's *laos* or people, a term usually reserved for Israel.[28] In the end, James declares, "We shouldn't create problems for Gentiles who turn to God."[29] It is a momentous decision, a watershed moment for the history of the church. Gentile converts do not have to be circumcised; they do not, in other words, have to become Jews in order to be Christians. This is the capstone to that earlier pronouncement that in Antioch the disciples were first called Christians. It means that the "mother church," represented here in the person of James the Just, has acknowledged that the new faith really is more than a Jewish sect.

James is not quite finished, however. Although he does not wish to "trouble" Gentile followers of Jesus, he does call on them to avoid four things that would be particularly odious to pious Jews and many Jewish Christians: things polluted by idols, fornication, whatever has been strangled, and blood. An unusual list, we might say at first glance. Yet it is a telling list when we take into account that all four prohibitions involve ritual concerns. Three of the four concern dietary issues. Meat offered in the sacrifices to false deities remained an ongoing issue that Paul would address elsewhere.[30] The third and fourth items are grounded in the Jewish belief that blood was sacred, and so the consumption of anything that still had blood in it (if it had been strangled, for instance) was forbidden. The mention of "fornication" in this list, while seemingly the odd one out given its focus not on food but on sexuality, nevertheless fits with the others inasmuch as it seems to represent a specific issue of sexual impropriety, namely something like temple prostitution.[31] A benefactor with a strong devotion to his household god or goddess might invite a client, who happens to be a Christian, to his house for dinner. That would most likely mean serving food that had been dedicated to the patron's deity and possibly could also involve after-dinner enticements with a temple "worker." For any follower of Christ, this could all be a bit awkward, but for those brought up in the Jewish tradition, it was the epitome of all that was most repugnant in the outside world. James clearly is trying to prevent his Jewish constituency in the church from deserting or otherwise rebelling.

James's decision is well received by all who are present for the Jerusalem Council. Note that even before this, Jewish and Gentile followers of Jesus alike agreed that they should honor crucial ethical directives like those found in the Decalogue. The problem did not lie here. It was not a matter of convincing Gentile believers that they should refrain from adultery or stealing, moral precepts that were already clear. No, what James does in one fell stroke is declare that the Jewish members of the church will accommodate the Gentile converts, while at the same time calling on the Gentiles to honor Jewish sensitivities about retaining their heritage and identity. It is a most gracious and carefully considered solution, one that Paul and Barnabas can live with for the time being. After all, at the heart of the decision is the underlying premise that one's identity as a Christian trumps one's identity as a Jew.

Of course, for some Jewish followers of Christ, all this is too much to take. As we will see next chapter, some instead continue to perpetuate the boundaries by refusing to eat with Gentiles. And when even Barnabas joins in, a remarkable partnership is severed.

74

All Things to All People

The popular image of Paul as a stern, uncompromising tyrant is far from accurate. True, before his conversion Paul recognized the power of Christ to break down all barriers, all boundaries between people, and he reacted with fear and dread at all that might be lost. In saying yes to Christ, Paul then did all in his power to help break down those barriers and build bridges. Barnabas, by welcoming him and training him in the face of others' resistance, showed the way. Paul replicated this model with the many disciples he helped bring along. In this way, he became the ultimate accommodator.

Nowhere do we see this more than in his first letter to the Christians in Corinth. On the one hand, he admits that "I act like a Jew to the Jews, so I can recruit Jews."[32] Luke shows a great example of this in Acts 21, when Paul later in his ministry again visits James and the elders in Jerusalem, and relates to them all of the incredible ministry being done among the Gentiles. Even as they praise God, we can sense their continued concern as they remind Paul of "thousands of Jews have become believers, and all of them keep the Law passionately."[33] They go on to relate how these zealous Jewish Christians have heard that "They have been informed that you teach all the Jews who live among the Gentiles to reject Moses, telling them not to circumcise their children nor to live according to our customs."[34] So they ask Paul to share in the rite of purification with four Jews who are under a vow, thereby showing that he still "live a life in keeping with the Law."[35] These elders reiterate the decision of the Jerusalem Council to welcome Gentiles without forcing circumcision on them, only asking for their pledge in turn to refrain from the list of particularly offensive acts. However, they clearly are trying to court the favorable opinion of their fellow Jews and Jewish Christians, and Paul accommodates and willingly submits to their request.

On the other hand, even as Paul is willing to become "as one under the law" to those who are themselves under the law, so too he shows himself to be more than willing to become as one "outside the Law" to win those who have little or no intention of being under the law. Indeed, he sums it all up by saying that he has "become all things to all people, so I could save some by all possible means."[36] Throughout the rest of that letter and in his other letters, Paul tries again and again to help his fellow Christians find ways to overcome their prejudices and predispositions, and make whatever accommodations are needed to help another feel welcomed. It was something he had learned from the best. Stephen the martyr taught Paul what it means to stand firm in one's convictions and be a soldier for truth. But Barnabas taught him how to reach out and be a steward of others. In the process, the church itself evolved and continued to become something new.

What Accommodations Are We Prepared to Make?

People in the first century found themselves face-to-face with changing realities all around them, and nowhere more than in the urban centers. In the face of change all around, it is understandable that many would cling to traditions, to all that is familiar, and resist the accommodations that were needed within the increasingly diverse faith communities that Paul and Barnabas were forming. For Jews and Jewish Christians, there were lines they did not want to cross, and changes they did not want to embrace.

For our congregations today, the challenge is similar. Whatever the location, size, or history of our churches, we share the reality that our "sacred bundle" is always subject to change. Now, that is a term that needs to be unpacked. The concept *sacred bundle* goes back to certain Native American tribes in which the shaman served as a carrier of a tangible leather bundle containing representational items—totems, symbols, icons—that defined the tribe's identity and purpose. From time to time, it was important to have the carrier of the bundle bring together the elders and people of the tribe, and then carefully, methodically open the bundle. One by one, the carrier would reveal each item for all to see, sharing the stories about why that item was important, what it said about the tribe's identity and purpose for existence. In each case, this was cause for celebration and honor, but in each case, there was also the possibility to lift up something and then with great care put it aside, so as to make room in the bundle for a new essential item. Far from being chaotic, by doing this periodically, the tribe avoided the twin temptations of either retaining everything with no regards for changing contexts and circumstances and needs, or throwing out the entire bundle and starting over every few years, which is chaos. No, by examining the contents of the bundle, by exploring the aspects of identity and purpose considered essential, sacred, the tribe was able both to stay connected to its rich heritage and adapt to the future as needed.

Congregations and their leaders would do well to consider their own sacred bundles and look carefully at that handful of crucial things that make them who and what they are. This can be a process over a period of several months, beginning with the clergy and lay leaders commissioning a task force to study the history of the congregation, with an eye to what their bundle looked like at the time of the church's founding, and how it had changed and evolved through the years. They could then name the things that they believe to be the essentials now and ask whether there should be any items that are lifted up in honor and then removed and if there are any items not yet in the bundle that need to be added. Then, the entire congregation can be brought together for a series of teachings and fellowship opportunities, perhaps as part of the Lenten season or at some other opportune time, in order to be included in the conversations about what has been essential and what needs to be essential moving forward. And all this happens with an eye toward the newer members and the outside community. A wise person once asked, "If your church disappeared tomorrow, who would notice or care?" It is a profound question about congregational identity and purpose, and it would serve us well to take the time to ask. The Council of Jerusalem was a watershed moment that resulted in a decision grounded in the appreciation of both continuity and change. To honor our heritage while making accommodations for the ever-evolving landscape around us is not easy, but it is work that we can—and, indeed, should—do, for the glory of God and the good of God's people.

Discussion Questions

1. This chapter opens with a story of a cross-cultural encounter. Share a time when you have had an experience with someone from a different culture. What was it like to reach out across cultural boundaries?

2. The shift from "Barnabas and Saul" to "Paul and Barnabas" marks a significant change in the relationship between the former mentor

and apprentice. What do you think this was like for Barnabas? Have you experienced something like this?

3. Reaching out to outsiders is a key theme for Paul's ministry. Who are the "outsiders" with whom you and your congregation need to connect, and what are the obstacles you face in trying to do that?

4. The Council of Jerusalem is a watershed moment in the life of the church. What do you think of the solution offered by James? Was it the best way forward? If so, why? If not, why not?

5. What would you say is in your tribe/congregation's sacred bundle? What items might have comprised part of the bundle in earlier years but since have been removed? What has been added, and how easy (or not) was that addition?

Chapter 5

To Include or Not to Include

Moving beyond Legalism

It is their moment of triumph. Their work of inclusive evangelism and church-building has been given the stamp of approval needed from the leadership in Jerusalem. It is time for these partners in ministry to celebrate all that they have accomplished together. It is time to reaffirm their incredibly successful partnership. Instead, Paul and Barnabas become embroiled in an intense dispute and go their separate ways.

Why? After all they had been through, facing so many opponents side by side, why would they choose now to leave one another's company? And what does their split, and the reasons for it, say about each of them? The answers are not necessarily obvious. For one thing, there is the slightly confusing problem of two different accounts of the conflict: the one in Acts 15 and the other in the second chapter of Paul's letter to the Galatians. More important, we may find that whatever assumptions we still have, about Paul in particular, may get in the way of appreciating the more complex reality behind the climatic battle of Barnabas versus Paul.

Barnabas vs. Paul: The Conflict in Acts

Just as the stoning of Stephen marked a significant transition earlier in Acts, so does the Council of Jerusalem serve as a turning point, indeed the key turning point. It marks the end of phase one of the mission to the Gentiles. It was Stephen's death, we are told, that resulted in a forced dispersion of the followers of Jesus, who went on to settle in places far from Jerusalem and the shadow of the temple, sharing their message with everyone they met. At the Council the foundation for the Gentiles' inclusion was set up and affirmed. However, it also marks the beginning of phase two of that same mission, with Paul and a new set of companions moving forward with an even greater boldness and taking the gospel to Rome, the heart of the empire, gateway to "the ends of the earth." It is somewhat surprising, therefore, to read the account of the decisive events in Jerusalem and the duo's return to their home base of Antioch, only then to turn to the following:

> Some time later, Paul said to Barnabas, "Let's go back and visit all the brothers and sisters in every city where we preached the Lord's word. Let's see how they are doing." Barnabas wanted to take John Mark with them. Paul insisted that they shouldn't take him along, since he had deserted them in Pamphylia and hadn't continued with them in their work. Their argument became so intense that they went their separate ways. Barnabas took Mark and sailed to Cyprus. Paul chose Silas and left, entrusted by the brothers and sisters to the Lord's grace. He traveled through Syria and Cilicia, strengthening the churches.[1]

After some time back in Antioch—the place where the two first came years before as mentor and apprentice, the place from where they were subsequently sent out as the church's ambassadors on their first apostolic journey—the two agree to return to the communities that they had established and see their progress. On this, the two agree. The disagreement comes when Barnabas suggests that they bring along John Mark—who had left them on their earlier mission. Paul vehemently refuses. And the two part company. It is that simple . . . and it is that complicated.

To understand this situation, it is helpful to consider the young man at the heart of this disagreement. I say "young man" because that is exactly how John Mark has been pictured through the centuries. Earlier in Acts, we hear of a house church based in the home of a woman named Mary, "Mary was John's mother; he was also known as Mark."[2] It was to this home that Peter made his way when, with some angelic assistance, he escaped from prison. The believers gathered there were both faithful and loyal, as is evident in their fervent prayers for Peter's sake. Interestingly, John Mark would forever become associated with "the Rock" of Jerusalem, as in the so-called first letter of Peter—an epistle attributed to the apostle though more likely a pseudonymous work written after his death—the author mentions Mark affectionately as his son in the faith.[3] It has been proposed that the second canonical Gospel (chronologically the first to be written), from which Matthew's and Luke's accounts draw much of their foundational material, was Mark's record of the story of Jesus as recollected by Peter.

It has even been argued by some that John Mark is the unnamed young man in the garden of Gethsemane at the time of Jesus's arrest who, "wearing nothing but a linen cloth," is himself suddenly apprehended, only to escape, leaving behind his scant covering and running off naked.[4] Not included in the other three canonical Gospels, it is such a unique and otherwise irrelevant tale (as it does nothing to further the narrative of Jesus's passion) that some have suggested that it is an autobiographical addition to the otherwise anonymous work. Whatever the facts behind this, and the rest of the tradition of Mark being a protégé of Peter's, the connection is an intriguing one, and might provide a bridge between the story of the conflict between Paul and Barnabas in Acts and Paul's own version in Galatians. But more on that in a moment.

For now, we should take note of John Mark's other familial connection, as he is described elsewhere in the New Testament as Barnabas's kinsmen: "Aristarchus, my fellow prisoner, says hello to you. So does Mark, Barnabas' cousin."[5] It should be remembered that Barnabas brought John Mark along with himself and Paul on their first missionary journey, only to have the young man leave them and return home when they prepared to set sail from Cyprus and make their the way to Pamphylia and Pisidia. As mentioned already, Luke does not identify the reason for the young man's abrupt departure. But it is neither irresponsible nor unreasonable to put on our detective hats and make some deductions based on what we do know.

First, we note that as John Mark is the cousin of Barnabas, it is not at all surprising that his older kinsman would take him under his wing. After all, Barnabas did this with Saul of Tarsus, in whom he saw great potential. How much more would he want to mentor his own relative! Indeed, this is exactly what we would expect of the Encourager.

Second, we might well infer that John Mark is an active follower of Jesus, given the fact that his mother's home had been the base for a house church, and that Mary is distinctly mentioned as being the mother of John Mark, a name known to Luke's readers.

Third, we know that this particular house church had strong connections with Simon Peter, as that is where he went as soon as he escaped from jail. It is not too much of a stretch, then, to suggest that the son of Mary, in whose house the church met, likely had some contact with Peter.

Fourth, although health concerns were earlier mentioned as one possible reason for his departure from Barnabas and Paul, John Mark is named much later in letters attributed to Paul and to Peter, and there is never any mention of health problems or recovery from health problems. Certainly he could have had a health concern back at the time that he left the group, but wouldn't Paul have shown a bit more compassion when John Mark had to return home for rest and recovery? The fact that this is even considered as a reason for his departure reveals an assumption that Paul was quite unsympathetic.

Indeed, the working assumption of so many people in all of this is that Paul is a harsh, uncaring taskmaster, concerned more about the work than people. In this scenario, Barnabas is set up as a kind of foil to Paul. While Barnabas is willing to let go of old grudges and show encouragement and care, especially given that John Mark is his cousin, Paul remains confrontational and unforgiving. The great danger here is that these are assumptions that we might bring to the situation, based on centuries of prejudices against Paul. When we look at Paul's own words to the Galatian Christians, we might find that we need to reevaluate our assumptions about the conflict and the motivations behind it.

Barnabas vs. Paul: The Conflict in Galatians

As mentioned above, when we move to Galatians, we see a very different account of the conflict:

> But when Cephas came to Antioch, I opposed him to his face, because he was wrong. He had been eating with the Gentiles before certain people came from James. But when they came, he began to back out and separate himself, because he was afraid of the people who promoted circumcision.

And the rest of the Jews also joined him in this hypocrisy so that even
Barnabas got carried away with them in their hypocrisy. But when I saw
that they weren't acting consistently with the truth of the gospel, I said to
Cephas in front of everyone, "If you, though you're a Jew, live like a Gentile
and not like a Jew, how can you require the Gentiles to live like Jews?"[6]

Here, whatever issue Paul has with Barnabas is corollary to his primary battle
with Peter. This in itself is fascinating and, for some, surprising, given that
the two chief apostles share a feast day in the Christian calendar and have
churches named after the two of them, including the National Cathedral.[7]
They both ended up in Rome, where they were martyred, and their names
thereafter have been forever linked, as early as the late first century by Clement of Rome in his letter to the Corinthians.[8] It is understandable that many
may think of Peter and Paul as being in sync. But, again, they would be
wrong.

Let's consider the context of the passage above. On the whole Galatians
stands out among all of Paul's letters, in stark contrast to the letter that chronologically precedes it. First Thessalonians, the very first of Paul's missives,
provides a kind of template for letter-writing that he follows thereafter. It
begins with an opening salutation: "From Paul, Silvanus, and Timothy. To
the Thessalonians' church that is in God the Father and the Lord Jesus Christ.
Grace and peace to all of you." Subsequent letters build on this brief formula,
usually offering an adjective of some kind to define Paul. The opening salutation is followed by a passage of thanksgiving for the community of believers
to whom Paul writes, commenting on their faith, love, and hope. Then comes
the body of the letter, which can be quite lengthy as in Romans, or only one
chapter total as in Philemon. Finally, there are closing comments and personal
greetings that further cement the bond between Paul and his initial readers.
This template—salutation, thanksgiving, body, and greetings—makes its way
throughout the canon of Paul's writings. The single greatest departure from it
is, no surprise, the letter to the Galatians.

From the outset, it is clear that Paul is facing considerable opposition
within the churches in Galatia.[9] Why else would he not only identify himself
as "Paul, an apostle," but go out of his way to assert that his apostleship is of
divine, not human origin? It is not as if he is personally unknown to these

people, as is the case with his letter to the Romans, for Acts records that on their first apostolic journey Barnabas and he traversed the various cities and areas that make up Galatia, setting up house churches in towns such as Derbe, Lystra, Iconium, and Pisidian Antioch. He knew these Christians, and they knew him. But now he opens his letter with the strongest possible language, affirming his authority as an apostle "not sent from human authority or commissioned through human agency."[10]

What is far more startling is that Galatians is the one letter—the only one out of all his letters—in which Paul does not include a thanksgiving section. While this may not at first glance appear remarkable, let me assure you that it is! Even in 1 Corinthians, where there were so many problems and divisions, the apostle somehow found a way to give thanks to God for them. Not so in Galatians. Indeed, in lieu of a thanksgiving, Paul instead includes a strong reproof section immediately following the salutation: "I'm amazed that you are so quickly deserting the one who called you by the grace of Christ to follow another gospel."[11] He goes on to blame those who "are confusing you and they want to change the gospel of Christ," and even goes so far as to condemn such a person twice: "They should be under a curse. I'm repeating what we've said before . . . they should be under a curse!"[12]

These are fighting words! And it says something about the strength of these opponents' influence over the Galatians that Paul appears very much to be on the defensive, fighting with everything he has to vindicate not only his apostleship (as mentioned already), but even more the core of the gospel message itself. Consider his accusation that they are trying to "change the gospel," or as other translations such as the NRSV put it, "pervert the gospel." The Greek word that Paul uses literally means to transform something to the opposite of what it is. Paul laments that by deserting him as their leader, they are "deserting the one who called you by the grace of Christ to follow another gospel."[13] This different gospel, this perverted gospel, is the opposite of what Paul introduced to them when he first came, which was a gospel of *grace*. And what was this perverted, opposite gospel that his opponents were peddling? They were insisting that converts must be circumcised, thereby becoming adherents of the Jewish law. In other words, it is the same old battle for Paul, the one he thought had been won once for all at the Jerusalem Council. But clearly he was wrong.

How demoralizing this must have been, how utterly disheartening! So much work, so much effort, now being undone and even reversed. It is difficult, perhaps impossible, for us today to recognize what a setback this was, or to appreciate what exactly was at stake. The primary issue was one of identity, of definition and belonging. To the Judaizers who came to the Galatian towns and stirred up the believers there, Paul was a dangerous man and his message was leading these converts away from the path of belonging to God's chosen people. These opponents were purists, insisting that circumcision coupled with subsequent adherence to the moral and ritual laws of Judaism was the prerequisite to inclusion in the Christian community. One's primary identity, then, remained that of a Jew, albeit a Jew who believed in Jesus as the promised Messiah. It was only logical from their standpoint that an uncircumcised Gentile Christian was an oxymoron. As for the decision of the Council, the fact that James the Just had somehow been "taken in" by Paul and Barnabas's stories was simply evidence that more stringent tactics were called for. They had to tear Paul down. Circumcision was nonnegotiable.

It was equally nonnegotiable for Paul but for different reasons. Paul can relate to his opponents' zeal for their Jewish heritage and laws—he reminds the Galatians of his own zealous past—but he goes on to say that they are missing the essential piece. If Jesus is redeemer, he is redeemer of all. If unmerited, undeserved love from God is found in Jesus, then it is there for all. Indeed, this for Paul is the very definition of grace. To do anything to earn it negates it, makes it something it is not, perverts it. It is grace or it is something very different. To say that circumcision is still needed is to say that the grace found in Jesus is not enough. That is why he is bold enough to proclaim that it isn't about his ego. If anyone presents a different gospel, including Paul himself, there's a problem.

This is why Paul was so grateful for the Jerusalem Council. He speaks in the second chapter of Galatians of both the personal and the external reasons he went to Jerusalem. On the personal side, Paul speaks of a revelation, not elucidating further, but then admits to laying out before the "influential leaders" the message he had been sharing with the Gentiles, "to make sure that I wouldn't be working or that I hadn't worked for nothing."[14] For all Paul's supposed bravado, there is something of a need for validation here, for knowing that he really is on the right track, and that these leaders agree he is on the right track. Paul expresses complete confidence that all he needs is divine backing for his apostleship and goes on to assert more than once that he does not care at all about the status of the "influential leaders." But one might well paraphrase the Bard, "Methinks he doth protest too much." For it seems fairly clear that despite his nonchalance about the "influential leaders," Paul truly does desire their affirmation. And when they give it, when they acknowledge that he had been "given the responsibility to preach the gospel to the people who aren't circumcised, just as Peter had been to the circumcised,"[15] then Paul thinks the battle for Gentile inclusion is over and won.

All this brings us back to the passage in question . . . all this points to the conflict. Sometime after the Council, when Paul and Barnabas are back in Antioch, Peter comes into town. It is interesting how Paul goes back and forth in calling the Rock by his Aramaic name, Cephas, and the Greek version, Petros/Peter. In any case, Peter comes to Antioch and, like Paul and Barnabas, sits and eats with the Gentile members of the congregation. This changes, however, when representatives from James of Jerusalem enter the scene. What does Peter think about this? Perhaps James is checking up on him. Perhaps the ultraconservative Jewish Christians are trying to accuse Peter of going soft.

In any case, as soon as these representatives show up, Peter immediately ceases eating with the Gentile believers, "because he was afraid of the people who promoted circumcision."[16] Other Jewish members of the congregation follow suit, including Barnabas himself, who "got carried away with them in their hypocrisy."[17] All this is too much for Paul. And so he confronts Peter in front of them all. The timing of all this is crucial. The Jerusalem Council had affirmed the mission to the Gentiles, had affirmed that they could be baptized and follow Christ *without* undergoing circumcision and becoming adherents of the Jewish law. All that was asked was that they avoid certain obviously offending practices, as seen last chapter, and that they remember the poor (presumably poor members of the congregation in Jerusalem). Given Paul and Barnabas's enthusiastic reception of the Jerusalem edict, it is unthinkable that the Christians in Antioch are disobeying it. If this was the case, Peter, given his own dietary scruples, would not be eating with them in the first place. No, clearly the Antiochene Christians are just enjoying their usual table fellowship as members of Christ's body.

The fault, Paul asserts, lies with Peter's fears of offending the hardcore purists of the circumcision party, and herein lies the hypocrisy that infuriates Paul. These Gentile Christians have done nothing wrong. The church's leadership has recognized them as sisters and brothers in Christ. And now that same leadership, personified in Peter, is communicating a very different message. No matter what was said earlier, now the Gentile members experience for themselves that they really are not totally welcome, that they still are viewed in some way as unclean, as outside the pure fellowship of God's people. They may have been told that they are equal in Christ, but Peter's actions speak far more loudly. So perhaps this is to be their future: equal but separate. In truth, then, they are not equal at all; they are, when it comes down to it, *less than*.

And what of the Encourager? Paul's words, "even Barnabas," are perhaps some of the saddest in all the New Testament.[18] This was Paul's friend, his mentor, the one who vouched for him, who stood by him, when the so-called pillars of the church wanted nothing to do with him. This is the one who first brought Paul to Antioch and showed him a community unafraid to share the gospel with Gentiles as well as Jews, a community so inclusive that they became known by a new name altogether: Christians. This is the one who in humility stepped back and let Paul take center stage, and then faithfully stood with him against the ire of reactionaries every time they dared to reach out to Gentiles. This is not Peter. This is not James. This is Barnabas, for goodness' sake! And now the Encourager turns his back on the very folk he once welcomed. For Paul, it must have felt like a kick to the stomach, a betrayal of all that they had stood for together. With those words, "even Barnabas," we hear the anguish of a disillusioned friend and mark the beginning of the end of a partnership in ministry.

Barnabas vs. Paul: Fighting for the Underdog

Anyone who has ever argued, ever assumed, that Paul was the guardian of the status quo needs to reread the letter to the Galatians. Only then, perhaps, does the story of the split in Acts 15 begin to become clearer, and the character of Paul less of a caricature. For as we see in Paul's own account of the events in Antioch, far from perpetuating old patterns and prejudices, he took them on . . . and at great cost. It was not easy to stand up to Peter. It was not easy to defy James's emissaries. And it most certainly was not easy to do all this while his old friend and former mentor left him standing alone. But from the moment he first said yes to Jesus, Paul had fought for the underdog, and he wasn't about to stop.

Returning to Acts, let us examine the passage where Paul and Barnabas go their separate ways in light of what we have seen in Galatians. Inasmuch as the Acts passage about their split occurs at the tail end of their time in Antioch, we can begin to create a reasonable timeline of events that places Paul's tough stance of John Mark in a different light. The sequence is: (a) Paul and Barnabas go to the Jerusalem Council to defend their mission among the Gentiles; (b) they return to Antioch with James's favorable edict in hand; (c) Peter comes to Antioch and participates in table fellowship with the Gentile believers; (d) representatives from James of Jerusalem come to Antioch to check on the situation; (e) upon seeing these emissaries, Peter and others, including *even Barnabas*, withdraw from the Gentile believers; (f) Paul rebukes Peter in front of all; (g) after a period of time, Paul suggests to Barnabas that they leave Antioch and return to the congregations that they set up; (h) Barnabas counters by suggesting that his cousin, John Mark, accompany them on this return trip; (i) Paul refuses and the duo separate. But, let's add one more crucial piece: John Mark, as we have seen, not only previously left them on their earlier mission to the Gentiles but also has been strongly linked with Peter.

It is hardly wild conjecture, then, to imagine that when Peter chose to withdraw from the Gentile Christians upon the arrival of James's representatives, and Barnabas followed his lead, so too did John Mark, who has been connected with both and with the church in Jerusalem, and who had left Paul when the going got tough in direct relation to the work with Gentiles. If we entertain this possibility—which is quite reasonable, given what we see above—then it is reasonable to consider that Paul's reaction was more about caring for those who were being tossed aside by Peter, Barnabas, and John Mark, than about him being a mean and unforgiving taskmaster.

For Paul, the "task" really was always about people, not simply about a cause. In the days before his conversion, his chief concern was for the people of Israel whose lives and heritage he believed to be potentially in danger because of the Jesus movement. He wasn't simply some raving madman; as we have seen earlier, he heard Stephen for himself and agreed that the message the martyr proclaimed was a dangerous message—dangerous, that is, to the Jewish people who relied on their boundaries and regulations to survive as a people under the constant threat of assimilation or extinction. They were, for Paul, the underdogs, and he would stand up for them. Following his conversion, his concern was for the people whose lives were transformed by Jesus, Gentiles as well as Jews. Indeed, now the Gentiles who were coming into the church were the underdogs. As for the old boundaries and regulations he once held dear, Paul now knew that within the church these would simply create a separate, tiered system in which some would be fully accepted and others not. For Paul, there could be no second-class members in the body of Christ.

Peter's hypocrisy, therefore, was more than a momentary lapse of judgment. His actions were in fact hurting many people, reinforcing that they were not fully acceptable. And John Mark's earlier failure to stay the course when the battle for Gentile inclusion was heating up was likewise more than a simple mistake that could be swept under the rug. His actions, like Peter's, were hurting people, hurting the underdogs. As for Barnabas, perhaps it was Paul's affection for his dear friend that made him to want to look past his failure in Antioch, for he still invited Barnabas to join him on the next journey. Perhaps Paul wanted to get out of Antioch and put what happened behind the two of them, try to regain the partnership they had before. But not with John Mark!

The epilogue to the story is interesting as well. We are told that Barnabas took John Mark with him back to Cyprus. This geographical detail might slip by readers as unimportant, but remember that this is home for the Encourager, this is familiar territory. And then, like Peter and the rest of the Twelve, Barnabas steps into obscurity and is heard of no more. Paul, on the other hand, takes Silas—one of two colleagues assigned to go to Antioch with their team at the close of the Jerusalem Council—and departs for a quick assessment of the churches founded earlier before carrying on to new mission fields. It is Silas, and not Barnabas, who will go on to endure imprisonment

89

with Paul for the sake of the gospel. It is Silas, and not Barnabas, who will go on to be included with Paul as opponents warn a town that "these people who have been disturbing the peace throughout the empire have also come here."[19] It is Silas, and not Barnabas, who is a co-author of the first of Paul's letters: "From Paul, Silvanus, and Timothy. To the Thessalonians' church,"[20] just as Timothy, who joins Paul soon after the split with Barnabas, is also named as co-author of some other epistles.[21] Far from being antisocial, or someone people would not want to be around, Paul would find himself colleagues and friends throughout his ministry.

One such companion is a Macedonian from Thessalonica named Aristarchus. He is first named as one of Paul's colleagues who is seized by an angry mob in Ephesus, and then accompanies Paul on later journeys, including to Rome.[22] But what makes him particularly noteworthy is when Paul mentions him personally in his later letters, along with a companion: "Epaphras, who is in prison with me for the cause of Christ Jesus, greets you, as well as my coworkers Mark, Aristarchus, Demas, and Luke," and again: "Aristarchus, my fellow prisoner, says hello to you. So does Mark, Barnabas' cousin . . . if he comes to you, welcome him."[23] Yes, that is indeed John Mark, a fellow worker at last!

Clearly, in later years Paul and John Mark have found common ground, but it is not because Paul has simply mellowed or become nicer, as some have suggested. Such comments assume yet again that earlier he was some unforgiving curmudgeon, that he put causes before people. No, to Paul the gospel is all about people, indeed about *all* people, not just those who think they alone are better because of their pedigree. The story of the split in Acts 15 is, in the end, not about Paul choosing confrontation over encouragement. It is not about mean Paul holding a grudge while nice Barnabas holds his arms open wide. No, it is about Barnabas and John Mark and good-old beloved Peter refusing to open their arms wide to all those Gentile Christians who had trusted them, who had taken them at their word that in Christ all are welcome, circumcised and uncircumcised alike. Paul has paid a high price through the years because he chose to welcome unconditionally when the other leaders hypocritically stood aloof. He chose to stay at the table of fellowship when others got up and walked away. He stood by his friends and fellow believers, because that is the right thing to do. After all, that was what he had learned years before from the very best of mentors.

Antioch Today

As said at the start, the issue of circumcision is not even on our radar today, and so it is very hard to realize all that was at stake back in Antioch. Yet we do understand quite well the emotions and biases and hurts that accompanied that conflict. How many times have we experienced, on both the local and larger levels, the kind of hypocrisy that Paul tackled head on. Perhaps we have sung the hymn, "All Are Welcome in this Place," while knowing that *those people*, whoever they are, are not really welcome at all.

For Paul, there was only one reality: "if anyone is in Christ, that person is part of the new creation. The old things have gone away, and look, new things have arrived!"[24] And elsewhere, his baptismal formula says it all: "There is neither Jew nor Greek; there is neither slave nor free; nor is there male and female, for you are all one in Christ Jesus."[25] In the next two chapters, we will consider how Paul dealt with those latter two categories: male/female and slave/free. For now, we have caught a glimpse of how hard he fought for the underdogs, and nowhere is that more evident than in his willingness to stand up for the Gentile believers in Antioch when others around him, *even Barnabas*, cast them aside. In this way, Paul made sure that the good words that came out of the Jerusalem Council were matched by good actions.

The Episcopal Church's 1979 *Book of Common Prayer* gave a high priority to the Baptismal Covenant. In the service for Holy Baptism, the team that worked on that prayer book followed past revisers and included the Apostles' Creed in a question-and-answer format as the foundational statement of faith. But they went further and added five questions about how we live out our faith. These questions force us to look in the mirror and see if what we do matches what we say we believe. "Will you strive for justice and peace among all people, and respect the dignity of every human being?" Our answer to this and the other questions is, "I will, with God's help." Without God's help, it would be impossible to move beyond our prejudices, our predispositions. But even with God's help, we must intentionally choose to stand for those who are regarded as *less than*, especially when others around us perpetuate the

91

prejudices. Some of those others may be people we have long respected and admired. Both then and now, it takes moral courage and intentionality to be a church that goes beyond lip service and legalism.

But how do we actually do this? One simple but effective way is to pull out our sacred bundle, discussed at the end of last chapter, and then have the parish leadership examine the ways in which the structures of our congregation either reflect that bundle or reveal a disconnect between what we say we are about and what we really do. Specifically, we look at four essential areas:

First, we look at our church budget and ask if we are indeed putting our money into the areas that we say are our priorities. No one in this day and age would fault us for not being able to do everything with the financial resources we have. But are the expenditures we do have matching the essentials that make up the bundle?

Second, we examine our facilities, our use of space, in light of the bundle's priorities. I have often heard parish leaders speak of youth and children being part of their bundle, key elements in the life of the parish. So I immediately ask not only for copy of their budget but also for the weekly calendar that shows how the church buildings are being used Monday through Saturday. In so many instances, I have seen a total disconnect between the way the facilities were being used daily and the bundle itself.

Third, we consider the choice of programming, ranging from the varieties of worship services on weekends to the educational forums and social offerings held throughout the week. Do the various services and programs fit our overall sense of what the congregation is called to do and be?

Fourth, we look at our use of human resources, meaning both paid staff and volunteers, and ask whether they are being utilized in ways to fit our vision and identity. Again, using the hypothetical case of a parish saying that youth and children are in their sacred bundle, we can see if adequate human resources are being allocated towards that.

When we consider these four structural markers together, we can gauge whether we are being honest with ourselves regarding our identity and our purpose, our sacred bundle. It is like using the five "action questions" at the end of the Baptismal Covenant to show us how we are living into what we profess in the Creed. This congregation we call our spiritual home is our

Antioch, and we can test how serious we are about the unity and equal value we share in Christ by asking if we are willing to sit at the table and dine with one another.

Discussion Questions

1. Finally, we see what the book's title has been hinting at, the breakup of one of the church's greatest partnerships. Have you ever seen such a split? Did the parties reconcile? Are there times when a separation is not really a bad thing?

2. Reread the Acts passage about the split between Paul and Barnabas, and the role John Mark played in it. What was your first reaction upon reading it? Now read it again: When have you been in Paul's position? In Barnabas's? In John Mark's?

3. Considering what was at stake in Galatia, what would have been the future of the Christian faith if the Judaizers ultimately had won? What might the church look like today if Paul had lost the battle?

4. When Peter and Barnabas stepped away from the table of fellowship, they did so out of fear. How do we let fear get in the way of our mission and fellowship in Jesus's name today?

5. Paul fights for the underdog, even at great cost to himself and the end of his partnership with Barnabas. Who are the underdogs in your community? What are the potential costs if we fight on their behalf?

Chapter 6
Neither Male nor Female
Moving beyond Gender Discrimination

The women should be quiet during the meeting. They are not allowed to talk. Instead, they need to get under control, just as the Law says."[1] Or, as another translation puts it, "Women should be silent in the churches. For they are not permitted to speak, but should be subordinate."[2] Few words have proven more damning to a person's reputation. Ask almost anyone today what they know about Paul, and odds are they will say something about his negative attitude toward women. If they are supporters of Paul, they might apologetically concede that he was simply a product of the time, that he was simply reflecting societal attitudes of that period. If they are not supporters, they will rake him over the coals, arguing that he contributed to the patriarchal discrimination and sexism that have plagued women ever since. What very few do is to dig a little deeper and find out for themselves what Paul actually said, *and perhaps did not say*, about women. For those willing to undertake this detective work, the results might be downright surprising.

Perhaps more so than anything that has already been said about Paul in this book, what follows in this chapter is a radical game changer for how we approach the apostle and how we understand his message. As will be argued here, while Paul clearly fought for the full inclusion of Gentiles in the body of Christ, he *assumed* the equality of women in ministry and leadership, and this in a time when wives were unnamed helpers in the shadow of their husbands. This is what made the man from Tarsus so very dangerous, so that his breath

95

had barely left his body when some leaders in the church began to revise or edit his more controversial views, especially about women. But don't take my word for it: be a detective, examine the following, and decide for yourself about Paul and women.

Women at Work in Acts

It is no secret that women living in the time of Barnabas and Paul did not have it easy. Relegated to a subordinate role in a predominately patriarchal culture, they lacked opportunities afforded to men and were often simply invisible companions to their fathers or husbands.

Yet in Luke's Gospel, we find numerous examples of women stepping into the spotlight and illustrating their worth—from Mary the mother of Jesus, who says yes to God's angelic messenger and braves societal censure, to Elizabeth her cousin and a prophetess in the temple, who recognize what others around them fail to see; from the widow of Nain who dares all for her child's life to an unnamed "sinner" who shows greater faith than the religious leaders who judge her; from the several women who financially support Jesus's ministry to one poor soul who gives all that she has to the temple coffers. And of course, there is Mary Magdalene, one of Jesus's financial backers, who as the first witness of the resurrection becomes "the apostle to the apostles," sharing the good news with his closest friends.

In Acts, Luke continues to lift up women and their contributions. In the opening chapter we find Jesus's own mother, listed alongside the reconstituted Twelve and other disciples in the upper room: "All were united in their devotion to prayer, along with some women, including Mary the mother of Jesus, and his brothers."[3] The next one is hardly an exemplar of goodness. In Acts 5, Sapphira joins her husband Ananias in trying to pull a fast one on the Jerusalem community and its leaders, only to find her own life forfeit.[4] Peter, who deals with Sapphira, finds a far stronger disciple in Tabitha of Joppa, also known as Dorcas, a woman whose life "overflowed with good works and compassionate acts on behalf of those in need" who becomes ill and dies, only to be brought back to life by Peter.[5] Two more women listed in Acts are Mary, the mother of John Mark (cousin to Barnabas), who sponsors a house church in her home, and a maid named Rhoda, who proves a bit overenthusiastic upon encountering a fresh-out-of-prison Peter at the house gate.[6]

The remaining women named in Acts are worthy of our attention, as all appear to be colleagues of Paul. The first is Lydia, "a Gentile God-worshipper from the city of Thyatira, a dealer in purple cloth," whose heart is opened by God upon hearing Paul speak and who, upon being baptized along her household, opens her home to the apostle and his companions.[7] It is interesting to note that although Luke mentions that she is married, we are not given the name of her husband, though we are given those several details above about her. Another is Damaris, a resident of Athens who joins Paul and becomes a believer, after hearing him preach in front of the Areopagus.[8]

The next woman on the list proves to be one of Paul's most highly valued coworkers: Prisca, or as she is affectionately referred, Priscilla. We first encounter her in Acts 18, when Paul arrives in Corinth: "There he found a Jew named Aquila, a native of Pontus. He had recently come from Italy with his wife Priscilla because Claudius had ordered all Jews to leave Rome. Paul visited with them. Because they practiced the same trade, he stayed and worked with them. They all worked with leather."[9] Several pieces of information about Priscilla are found in this brief introduction. We learn that she is married to Aquila, a Jew and native of Pontus in Asia Minor. The couple was expelled from the imperial capital by the edict of Claudius in the year 49 CE, making their way to Corinth to begin a new life.[10] We learn that they are leatherworkers, tentmakers, part of a trade that Paul shared with them. (We might call this an early version of bivocational ministry.) We see the couple's generous hospitality towards Paul, opening their home to him. Not long thereafter, we see them reaching out to a naïve evangelist, Apollos, training him in the Christian faith, and then accompanying Paul on another apostolic journey, eventually staying in Ephesus, where they open their home as a gathering place for Christians.

Do note that Priscilla's husband, Aquila, is never mentioned alone, but always with her, and in fact two-thirds of the time Priscilla is named first! This is not a small thing. In the first century, it would have been unusual to do this, and therefore speaks well of Priscilla's gifts and the high regard in which she was held. Consider the contrast with two other wives named in Acts: Druscilla, the Jewish wife of Felix, the Roman governor of Judea, and Bernice, the wife of King Agrippa. Both are named along with their husbands, but both are named second.[11] Priscilla stands apart. In fact, there have been some scholars who suggest that she authored the anonymous Letter to the Hebrews in the New Testament. In any case, what is most remarkable in Luke's description of Priscilla, or Lydia for that matter, is what is *not* said about their contributions. There is *no* controversy about these women being collaborators in ministry. Paul makes *no* fuss about their roles. There is *no* mention by him of a need for these women to be silent.

And what he says in his own letters is even more noteworthy.

Equality of Service in Paul's Letters

In one of his earliest letters, the epistle to the Galatians, Paul responds to the claims of those demanding that circumcision, a Jewish rite of initiation, was necessary for a Gentile to enter the Christian community. In the midst of detailed response that focuses on the primacy of faith over law for all who would be children of Abraham, he interjects what many believe to be an early baptismal formula: "There is neither Jew nor Greek; there is neither slave nor free; nor is there male and female, for you are all one in Christ Jesus."[12] Whatever its origin, it is a reminder to each person who wishes to come into the church that within this community all outside divisions, distinctions, and dichotomies lose their meaning. To be "in Christ," as he says elsewhere, "that person is part of the new creation. The old things have gone away, and look, new things have arrived!"[13] All the things that seemed so important in the outside world mean nothing to those now inside the community of the redeemed. What is particularly interesting about this formula, however, is that it not only includes the irrelevance of a Jewish-Gentile contrast, but also one between men and women.

We certainly see this in terms of the people Paul includes among his co-workers. At the end of his letter to the Romans, for example, in his personal greetings to that church there Paul names several women doing significant work.[14] He begins with a formal commendation of Phoebe, a member of the church at Cenchreae, a seaport about eight miles from Corinth. She is described by Paul as a sister (in the faith) and a "servant" (the Greek *diakonos* is, literally, "deacon"). As Phoebe bears Paul's letter to the Christians in Rome, he directs them to give her whatever she needs as she has been a "sponsor" or patron of many, including Paul himself. Given that Paul has not yet visited Rome when he pens this epistle, it says much of Phoebe that he would entrust her with this carefully crafted introduction of himself and his theology to the church there.

Immediately following this commendation, he offers his greetings to believers whom he knows, beginning with our friends Prisca (the formal name of Priscilla) and Aquila, and again we see the wife listed first. They are both described as Paul's coworkers who have "risked their own necks" for him. Paul further notes that the couple is deserving not only of his thanks, but indeed of the gratitude of "all the churches of the Gentiles." And apparently by this time, Priscilla and Aquila have made their way from Ephesus to the imperial capital, as Paul mentions the house church there in their home.

Following this familiar couple, he also mentions Mary, "who has worked very hard for you." Later in the list of greetings he names three other women who have worked hard in the Lord: Tryphaena, Tryphosa, and finally Persis, who is also described as "my dear friend." It has been noted by scholars that, although Paul speaks of some men as fellow workers, the reference to exhausting or strenuous work is restricted to women. Julia, another woman, is named briefly towards the end of the greetings, as is one Paul intriguingly describes as Rufus's "mother and mine."[15]

Then Romans 16:7 presents the most controversial name in Paul's list: "Say hello to Andronicus and Junia, my relatives and my fellow prisoners. They are prominent among the apostles, and they were in Christ before me." These two are described as kinsmen of Paul's, or fellow Israelites, who became followers of Jesus before him and then endured prison with him. It has long been debated if the Greek *Junian* is to be understood as Junia, which is a woman's name, or Junias, a man's name. The reason for the controversy is that Paul goes on to speak of this person, along with Andronicus, as "prominent among the apostles." Surely this could not be a woman, some then argue. But arguing for it to be masculine is a bit of a stretch, both grammatically and because the person is listed alongside this Andronicus as if they are a couple, not unlike Prisca and Aquila. Patristic writers, those earliest Christian writers outside of the Bible, believed it to be Junia, a woman. The controversy itself, however, reveals how threatened some have been at the thought of Paul mentioning a woman as an apostle. How threatened? Read on.

Editing Paul

Now we come to the hard stuff! If indeed Paul included women among his coworkers, if he believed that in Christ there is no male and female, then why in the world would he tell women to be silent in church, as we saw at the start of this chapter? After all, he said some pretty discriminatory things about women and their role. Or did he?

In Paul's first letter to the Corinthian Christians, there are two notable sections that deal with women, or more to the point, that place strong restrictions on women. The more well-known passage is a two-verse piece found towards the end of chapter 14: "Like in all the churches of God's people, the women should be quiet during the meeting. They are not allowed to talk. Instead, they need to get under control, just as the Law says. If they want to learn something, they should ask their husbands at home. It is disgraceful for a woman to talk during the meeting."[16] Now these lines come at the end of a lengthy discussion about orderly worship, with the specific focus in chapter 14 being tongues, or ecstatic utterances, which apparently were fairly common in Corinthian worship. Paul's concern here is for visitors who will not comprehend what is going on in the service unless someone interprets the tongues. Likewise, any prophetic statements that are made should be done one at a time, so that there is time to absorb and consider what was being said. This is again for the sake of the uninitiated person who needs some order in the service. As Paul put it, "God isn't a God of disorder but of peace." This is verse 33. In verse 36, we pick up on this same train of thought: "Did the word of God originate with you?" and leads into more discussion about prophecy and tongues, concluding with a summary statement in verses 39-40: "So then, brothers and sisters, use your ambition to try to get the gift of prophecy, but don't prevent speaking in tongues. Everything should be done with dignity and in proper order."

Between verses 33 and 36 we have something of an interruption, as the focus turns abruptly from prophecy and tongues in worship to women keeping quiet. The effect is a little jarring. To the observant reader, it becomes even more interesting, as many modern English translations, such as the NRSV, contain a footnote at the bottom of the page that says something like this: "Other ancient authorities put verses 34-35 after verse 40." This means that the lines about restrictions on women speaking were not even in the same place in the earliest manuscripts. Remember, the books of the Bible did not suddenly drop down from the sky but were written by people like Paul and then reproduced by various unknown copyists. While we do not have the apostle's actual original letter, what we do have are several early copies, which almost always agree with one another. This is one of those rare instances where the texts do not agree. Some have these words about women in one place, breaking up the train of thought about tongues and prophecy, and others in another place, at the end following a clear closing summary. Neither location really works, as they bring more confusion than sense to the surrounding context. To add to the mystery, a recently uncovered very early manuscript does not contain the controversial verses in either place. Instead, they are found in the margins of the page!

All this is fascinating enough. But then we can also add the fact that the vocabulary in these verses is quite different from Paul's language in the rest of the book or even elsewhere in his letters. "Just as the law says" is a very un-Pauline thing to say. So, too, is the phrase "in all the churches," or the words "get under control" and "disgraceful."[17] The result is a questionable section being attributed to Paul. Where we *do* see similar vocabulary is in chapter 11 of the same letter, which, interestingly, also offers a fairly negative set of options for women.

There, in 1 Corinthians 11, Paul opens another section on worship in verse 2: "I praise you because you remember all my instructions, and you hold on to the traditions exactly as I handed them on to you." Verse 17 appears to continue this thought: "Now I don't praise you as I give the following instruction because when you meet together, it does more harm than good." As is hopefully clear, there is a logical train of thought between these two verses: "I praise you . . . but in the following I do not praise you." What follows is a pastoral directive on why the wealthier members of the church should wait for the working class to come in from their duties before beginning their communal feast, which included the Eucharist. The passage culminates with verse 33: "For these reasons, my brothers and sisters, when you get together to eat, wait for each other." All of this is fairly clear and makes sense.

But between verses 2 and 17, we find a confusing passage about women needing to cover their heads in worship. I say confusing because it breaks up the train of thought about showing concern for others above one's own self, especially when it comes to the communal meal. I say confusing also because the vocabulary in this section is unlike Paul's language in the rest of the letter or elsewhere, except in the verses in chapter 14 as mentioned already. Here in chapter 11, we find talk about angels being scandalized by women having their heads unveiled or uncovered. The word used here for *veiling* is unique in Paul's writings. Why would he bring it up? Veiling was not something common in the surrounding culture, except for special occasions such as at times of marriage or mourning. Veiling was a custom among Jewish women, though more so in some places than in others. And, interestingly, it set them apart from their Gentile counterparts, who were unveiled. This means that, if Paul is indeed writing this, he is advocating a very specific Jewish ritual for his largely Gentile congregation, quite the opposite of his constant fight to prevent circumcision from becoming a requirement for male Gentile converts.

Paul's chief concern throughout 1 Corinthians is the unity of the people in the church, that they should honor one another, respect one another, and show love toward one another as fellow members of the body of Christ. The two sections dealing with restrictions on women—one of which is actually found in different places in different early manuscripts—do not fit with his overall argument, his specific train of thought in each section, or even his typical vocabulary. It should also come as little surprise that in chapter 12, where the baptismal formula from Galatians is again used—"Jews or Greeks, slaves or free"—the third pair, "male or female," is missing.[18] So, what are we to make of all this? One argument often used when questions are raised about this is that there was a group of particularly troublesome women in Corinth and Paul needed to deal with them, but again this does not explain the problems in placement and vocabulary mentioned above. It also does not fit Paul's clear acceptance of women in leadership as noted in his greetings at the end of Romans.

By now, it might be obvious what I am going to suggest. Perhaps, just perhaps, Paul did not write those problematic sections at all. Rather, I would argue that they were edited in very soon after his passing so as to deal with the challenge of women in positions of leadership and the threat they posed to the status quo. One efficient way that the next generation could deal with problems they were facing would be to invoke the name of the apostle in presenting a case for restricting women's roles and rights. Indeed, such tactics were not at all unusual in ancient writings.

What I am proposing is widely accepted when it comes to the disputed letters of Paul, those letters that use very different language and appear to address issues that arose after Paul's lifetime. Some truly are disputed, as scholars are divided in opinion about whether all or part of the letters to the Ephesians and the Colossians are truly written by Paul. The two are usually linked, largely because so many passages in Ephesians appear to be expansions or variations of passages in Colossians. Far from being a modern idea, the Dutch Renaissance scholar Erasmus questioned whether Paul wrote Ephesians, and many since have pointed to the letter's un-Pauline language and extremely long sentence structures unlike anything in the undisputed letters. And Colossians has been under scrutiny not only for its vocabulary but also for its content, as it appears to contend with issues and gnostic heresies that did not arise until the second century.

These two disputed epistles, along with the first letter attributed to the Apostle Peter, contain "household codes" in which wives are directed to "submit" to their husbands in everything, as to the Lord.[19] These codes are quite similar to household codes such as in Aristotle's *Politics*, even echoing the three sets of dominant/subordinate relational pairings: "Of household management we have see that there are three parts—one is the rule of a master over slaves . . . another of a father, and the third of a husband."[20] There are also strong similarities to Jewish philosophers like Philo, who speaks of the need for women to be subservient, and Josephus, who asserts that the woman is in all things inferior to the man. But the codes are notably different from the kind of talk that Paul uses in his "undisputed" letters like Galatians and Romans. (Later in the same codes, we see slaves directed to obey their earthly masters "with fear and trembling,"[21] a point that we will explore more in the next chapter.)

103

By the time we get to the so-called Pastoral Letters, the letters addressed to Timothy and Titus, a majority of scholars agree that they were written after Paul's death by someone else (though, especially in the case of 2 Timothy, with some excerpts of Paul's actual writing woven in). First Timothy 2 contains a section about how a woman should dress and act, so as to acknowledge her status as a subordinate, sounding very much like what we saw in those problematic verses in 1 Corinthians 14: "A wife should learn quietly with complete submission. I don't allow a wife to teach or to control her husband. Instead, she should be a quiet listener."[22] Someone clearly has a problem with women in leadership; the question—the crucial question—is whether that someone really is Paul!

Yet even as the Pastoral Letters were painting him as the keeper of the status quo, there were other writings around the same time period that offered a different picture. One such piece is the *Acts of Paul and Thecla*. While lesser known today, it was disseminated widely in the early church. In it, Paul is pictured as an ascetic figure, encouraging followers to take his example and avoid marriage. Thecla is a young zealous protégé of Paul. She preaches and baptizes, and eventually her adventures take her to the point of a probable martyr's death, only to find herself miraculously spared and reunited with her mentor. Now, it is not being suggested here that this represents a historical picture of Paul, but what is noteworthy is that this book does offer a different take on the apostle than that of the household codes, the Pastoral Letters, or the problematic passages found in 1 Corinthians. As in Acts and Romans, he clearly welcomes a coworker who happens to be a woman. This account was later denounced by no less a Christian authority than Tertullian in the late second century. Why? The reason is that he disapproved of the example it set for women to think they could preach and baptize.[23]

Recovering Paul

Paul, the fearless advocate for unity and equality in Christ as seen in Acts, in Galatians, in Romans, soon became known instead as the arch-conservative whose restrictions on women resulted in nineteen centuries of inequity. It appears that his opponents succeeded in the ultimate spin. If Paul could not be discredited as an apostle, then the next best option for those who feared what he set in motion was to rein things in and to do so under his name, to make it sound as if he demanded adherence to the social status quo. Their strategy worked. They found a way to domesticate the radical.

In earlier chapters, I have argued that because he was so radical, because he followed his mentor Barnabas in subverting the status quo instead of bolstering it, Paul was recognized as a threat. In other circumstances, the church's leadership might have found a way to accuse him, excommunicate him, even kill him. Any student of church history knows that I am not exaggerating. But this is the pioneer who blazed the trail and planted Christian communities wherever he went, who wrote letters that were shared throughout the various churches and lifted up as scripture.

Like Mary Magdalene, the "apostle to the apostles" who became known instead as a former prostitute, and like Francis of Assisi, the challenger of social and economic disparities who became known instead as an eccentric proto hippie, Paul the liberator, who recognized and affirmed the leadership gifts of colleagues who were women, went on to be canonized and put on a pedestal while at the same time his reputation was altered. Dorothy Day, founder of *The Catholic Worker* and fearless advocate for the vulnerable and the voiceless, said, "Don't call me a saint; I don't want to be dismissed so easily." Paul, no doubt, would agree.

Why, you may ask, do we need to worry about this? In answer to this, let me offer a bit of a history lesson. In my own Episcopal Church, on July 29, 1974, in "the city of brotherly love," a group of women known collectively as the "Philadelphia Eleven" were ordained to the priesthood,[24] an act that produced shock waves throughout the Church and the worldwide Anglican Communion of which The Episcopal Church is a part. Before this, women could be found in groups such as the Episcopal Church Women (ECW), Daughters of the King, and the Altar Guild, but usually not serving on vestries at that point and certainly not wearing clerical collars. The Philadelphia Eleven changed all this. Less than two years after their "irregular" ordinations, at the Church's 1976 General Convention, bishops and deputies debated and deliberated and ultimately affirmed that "it is now the intent of The Episcopal Church as an ecclesial community to authorize the ordination of women to the priesthood and to episcopal orders."[25] Ten years later, Barbara Harris would become the first woman consecrated to the episcopate, and twenty years after that event, Katharine Jefferts Schori would be elected by her fellow bishops and installed as the twenty-sixth Presiding Bishop of The Episcopal Church. Other denominations have likewise embraced women in clergy and lay leadership positions.

However, it was not long after these events when a small but vocal minority spoke out in opposition, with some in their number actually leaving the Church and others remaining but refusing to ordain women or allow them at work in their dioceses. And, two thousand years after Paul's time, the Roman Catholic Church and the Eastern Orthodox Churches still cling to an all-male priesthood, usually returning to the age-old argument that because the original apostles, meaning the Twelve, were male, then their ordained successors should be as well. Still other churchgoers in a variety of traditions cite Paul and the statements attributed to him as a defense for their bias against women in ordained, or even lay, leadership. We live in an age where women serve society as doctors and lawyers, as professors and scientists, as members of Congress and justices on the Supreme Court. And yet for many, the rules are different when it comes to leadership in churches. I recently chatted with someone who disapproved of women serving as ushers in the local parish and who, unsurprisingly, looked to Paul for support.

We must recover Paul in regards to the role of women.

The Lenses through Which We Read

Scholars refer to the "canon" of holy scripture, by which they mean the recognized, authoritative collection of biblical books. The letters of Ignatius of Antioch and that of Clement of Rome are well-respected, well-studied works that date to the same time period as some of the later books in the New Testament, and yet they are not considered part of the biblical canon. The famed sixteenth-century reformer, Martin Luther, had little regard for the Letter of James, which for various reasons he considered "an epistle of straw,"[26] but he could not excise it from the twenty-seven book New Testament, because the canon was so firmly established by that point. The biblical canon remains a yardstick, as it were, by which other writings, teachings, and doctrines are measured and judged.

The fact remains that the problematic passages about women considered here are indeed a part of the canon of scripture. They are part of the recognized, authoritative collection of biblical books, as are other problematic passages about everything from slavery to total war on civilian populations to polygamy. So how do we make sense of it all? As suggested before, the Bible is not meant to be ingested without thinking, like some kind of cotton candy that is sweet and easy to go down, but rather we must "read, mark, learn, and inwardly digest."[27] Scripture is something of substance that needs to be chewed on, wrestled with. One way to do this is to acknowledge that we all have our our own canon within the canon, verses or sections of scripture which influence the ways we understand the larger whole. In other words, just as we consider other writings and teachings by viewing them through the lens of scripture, so we approach the difficult parts of scripture by examining them through the lens of certain parts that are essential to us.

As an example, consider two statements of Jesus recorded in the Gospels: "Whoever isn't against us is with us," and "whoever isn't against you is for you."[28] Both are there, both are attributed to Jesus, but the emphasis of the first is on openness and welcome to the other, while the emphasis of the second is on caution and suspicion of the other. Depending on which statement we embrace as essential, we may approach other parts of scripture accordingly. Another example regards a biblical definition of sin and salvation. As time passed, the Western part of the church considered sin through the lens of Romans with its more legal jargon of transgression that requires punishment, while salvation is justification, or payment, for the crime. "God paid the price for us." In the Eastern Church, on the other hand, sin was viewed through the lens of Colossians with its view of the marring of the divine image in us, and salvation is deification, or having the icon that is each of us restored to allow God to shine through. "God became human so that human beings might become like God." Both are there, but with very different emphases that have played out in their respective ways in liturgy, in teachings, in worldviews.

Still another example concerns the central unifying theme of Paul. To Martin Luther, a medieval monk who felt great responsibility and guilt in his own life, the key piece in Paul's writings by which he read and understood all the rest was "justification by faith." In more recent years, some scholars have offered a new perspective, suggesting that the central theme in Paul's letters is more about the need for unity within the church, especially between Jews and Gentiles.[29] Now, both are there, but the two different emphases will lead to different ways of reading Paul.

And then we can also consider how we approach scripture through the lenses of our own life experiences and cultural context. An excellent report and resource guide produced in 2013 by the Anglican Communion Office, entitled *The Bible in the Life of the Church*, invited participants from several different parts of the world to engage the Bible using a common set of questions and discovered, perhaps unsurprisingly, the we do all approach scripture from the social and cultural context in which we live. Those steeped in a culture that places individualism at the apex of its values will read certain passages in a different way from those in a culture that is far more communally focused. These different contexts form another kind of a yardstick by which to read scripture, an experiential canon to interpret the canon.

Jesus himself was challenged by some crafty opponents to state which of the commandments he considered to be the greatest. Now, this was a not-so-subtle test, for with over nine hundred commandments in the Old Testament, the Hebrew scriptures, whichever he would choose would undoubtedly be challenged by his opponents: "Ah, but what about this other commandment?" As always, Jesus saw through their ruse and presented the perfect response, his canon within the canon: "*You must love the Lord your God with all your heart, with all your being, and with all your mind. This is the first and greatest commandment. And the second is like it: You must love your neighbor as you love yourself.*"[30]

So, returning to the issue of women, on the one hand we can interpret relevant passages through a lens of communal order and hierarchy, and on the other hand we can interpret them through a lens of the value of the individual and equality. We will come to different conclusions in the end, and what is then required is a mutual graciousness to hear and honor one another without necessarily agreeing. As former U.S. Secretary of State (and Episcopalian) Madeline Albright once said, "More and more, we make for ourselves a world of 'us' against 'them.' Instead of conspiring with the like-minded, we need to spend more time learning from those we consider wrongheaded."[31]

Perhaps one of the best examples of this in regards to different views of the leadership roles of women in the church may be found in the 1978 Lambeth Conference of Bishops, one of a series of gatherings every ten years of Anglican bishops throughout the world at the invitation of the Archbishop of Canterbury. Taking place a mere four years after the Philadelphia Eleven and two years after the 1976 General Convention of The Episcopal Church that made official the ordination of women, Lambeth 1978 produced a resolution that directly addressed the issue. While admitting that the ordinations had caused "distress and pain to many on both sides," these gathered bishops of the worldwide Communion acknowledged "the legal autonomy of each of its member Churches, with the legal right . . . to make its own decision about the appropriateness of admitting women to Holy Orders." Most significant here is the note that, while the actions of some member churches to ordain women to the priesthood "may disappoint" some of the communion's ecumenical partners, most notably the Roman Catholic Church and the Orthodox Churches, the bishops made it clear that "our holding together of diversity within a unity of faith and worship is part of the Anglican heritage."[32]

This is what Barnabas the Encourager did and what he mentored Paul to do as well. It is what Paul talks about again and again in his letters, as in 1 Corinthians when he urges the church members there to wait for one another, honor one another, love one another. We still have to contend with the fact that difficult and problematic passages about women remain in our canon of Holy Scripture. But *how* we read and interpret these passages will prove crucial. And in all of this, let us consider that perhaps Paul was so radical in his profession that in Christ there is neither male nor female, so egalitarian in his recognition of women as fellow workers, that those around him who preferred to keep women in a place of inferiority and subservience took steps to tamper with Paul's writings in order to edit his reputation and place the Great Liberator on the side of the misogynists.

Discussion Questions

1. "The women should be quiet during the meeting. They are not allowed to talk. Instead, they need to get under control, just as the Law says." What is your first reaction upon reading those words?

2. Priscilla and Aquila are shown in Acts to be in full partnership in ministry (in contrast to Ananias and Sapphira, who earlier are shown to be partners in crime). Consider a couple you know who inspire you in their shared mission.

3. Reread Romans 16 and list all the coworkers named by Paul. What do you learn by looking at this list? Why might he have mentioned these specific persons?

4. Taking the role of scriptural detective and looking again at the problematic passages about women in 1 Corinthians 11 and 14, what deductions do you make? Do you still believe that Paul wrote them? If so, how do they fit with Galatians 3:28 or Romans 16? If not, why do you think they were added?

5. What is your canon within the canon, that is, which verses or passages of scripture are most important to you and why?

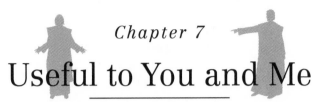

Chapter 7

Useful to You and Me

Moving beyond Social Disparities

P aul's epistle to the Christians in Rome is sixteen chapters in length, each chapter densely packed with theological substance. Countless volumes of commentaries and book studies have been devoted to this magnum opus through the centuries, and both professors and preachers wax eloquently on the truths found therein. Although one of the apostle's later writings, its size and its importance place it first in the Pauline correspondence. All the way at the other end of that epistolary collection is the tiny letter that Paul wrote to a Christian named Philemon. Only twenty-five verses in length, it rarely merits more than a passing mention in most discussions about the apostle. Some say that it only made it into the New Testament canon by being seemingly attached to the epistle to the Colossians, a kind of afterthought as it were.

And yet this overlooked treasure, written towards the end of his life during prison confinement, contains one of the most powerful summaries of Paul's understanding of the Christian identity, relational equality, and personal value. Paul's letter to Philemon is the most personal of all his writings and provides an invaluable glimpse into the mind and heart of a pastor and mentor. Although Barnabas is nowhere to be seen in these verses, his influence looms large, as his one-time protégé proves himself to be a great supporter of the underdog, in this case a seemingly useless runaway slave. And when Paul confronts the erstwhile slave owner, even then he does so in an encouraging way! If the church had paid attention to this little masterpiece,

111

history might have turned out very different. Instead, the Great Liberator was again ignored and then reinterpreted as the preserver of the status quo.

Networks of Dependence in Paul's Time

Before examining Paul's letter to Philemon, it is important to step back and briefly consider the big picture. Individualism as we understand it in the twentieth century was unknown in Paul's time, as one's identity was understood largely in terms of that person's relational networks. Many of these, in turn, were defined not by the equality of those involved but rather by the power differential between them. In the last chapter, we considered how the so-called household codes kept married women in a dependent, subservient role vis-à-vis their husbands, but those same codes also spoke about the "proper" relationship between children and their parents, and slaves and their masters.

There was also the relationship between business clients and their patrons, though these relationships were more like that of adult children to parents. The Roman statesman, Cato the Elder, once said, "While the foremost obligation is to a father, the next is to a patron."[1] Philo of Alexandria, the Hellenistic Jewish philosopher, expressed even more broadly the social gulf between elders, rulers, benefactors, and masters and younger people, subjects, clients, and slaves, with the former group being the "higher and superior class" deserving of the respect and obedience of the latter.[2] Consider the not-so-subtle accusation against Pontius Pilate by those who violently opposed his suggestion of leniency for Jesus: "If you release this man, you aren't a friend of the emperor!"[3] Caesar was the ultimate patron, as his "client," Pilate, was thus reminded. Of course, while every patron (except the emperor) was, in some way or another, a client to someone else, a slave served only one master, as Jesus himself once said.[4] And while a client could be identified as "the friend of" the patron, a slave was in actuality the property of his or her master, and the latter's rights over the slave were absolute.

The result was a careful balance in which the overall societal system remained intact as long as everyone's roles remained clear and loyalties were maintained. Those loyalties, especially of a slave to a master, took precedence over all other demands on a person's identity. A prime example of this, mentioned in an earlier chapter, is found in the Corinthians situation in which some church members were under pressure to eat meat offered in the pagan sacrifices, precisely because they were clients of a patron who expected such, and any refusal to do so would have been tantamount to throwing away all chances for social or professional advancement. Now, if this was true for a client, who at least had the choice in the midst of the pressure, for the slave, there could be no alternative whatsoever—except the one that Onesimus took, to run away.

There were exceptions and nuances to all that has just been said, of course. If we think again about the situation for women, widows often discovered a freedom heretofore unknown to them, as they could now have control over their deceased spouse's estate and make decisions that would have been unthinkable while their husband was alive and in obvious control. And a household servant or slave might enjoy considerable oversight of the family's finances or wield authority over young children, including in regards to their education. Of course, once those children came of age, they would outgrow the servant/slave's authority, and the "lines of reporting," as we might now call them, would irrevocably be reversed. It is interesting today to watch television episodes of *Downton Abbey* or *Upstairs, Downstairs*, which reveal similar networks of dependence, with their own occasional exceptions and nuances, albeit in the cultural context of the declining British Empire. The world that Paul inhabited was, of course, different in many ways from twentieth-century England, but not wholly unfamiliar.

In the midst of all this, the danger for the church was that it could end up becoming one more relational network, one more group, among all the others that placed demands on the lives of first-century people. What Paul, first with Barnabas and then later without him, tried to help people see is that believing and belonging in Christ trumped all other demands, including in the various networks of dependence. For Christians living in that time, theirs was a world of multiple overlapping and competing relational networks . . . but Paul was calling them to something not of this world.

The Case of Onesimus

We turn now to the specific case of an imprisoned Paul vouching for a runaway slave in his letter to Philemon. First, note the way Paul describes himself in the salutation. It should be remembered that in Galatians and the Corinthian correspondence, he used the self-descriptor of "apostle," inasmuch as he was addressing challenges to his authority in those churches. In his letter to the Philippians, he used the less authoritative term, "slave,"[5] which both fit his affectionate relationship with that community and also foreshadowed his discussion about the need for a spirit of humility and self-emptying, as Christ "he humbled himself by becoming obedient to the point of death, even death on a cross."[6] Here instead, in Philemon, Paul describes himself as a "prisoner." Given that Philemon and the church in his house undoubtedly are aware of Paul's incarceration, it seems at first glance as if he is simply stating the obvious. But, as always, Paul is a wordsmith for whom every syllable counts. In this case, the self-designator is a reminder that it is quite literally for their sake that Paul is in prison. His "crime" was proclaiming the gospel to Gentiles like them as well as to Jews. Philemon and his fellow Christians are indeed indebted to Paul.

As in the majority of his letters, Paul is not alone in addressing this group. Timothy is with him. As noted in an earlier chapter, this son of mixed marriage—he had a Greek father and a Jewish mother who was a person of "authentic faith"[7]—came into Paul's life immediately following his split with Barnabas. Along with Silas, Timothy endures hardship and imprisonment alongside Paul, and on several occasions serves as an ambassador for the apostle, a trusted go-between with the churches.[8] He is named as a co-author in many of Paul's letters, including 1 Thessalonians, 2 Corinthians, and Philippians, as well as Colossians and 2 Thessalonians, and is even named as the recipient of two letters attributed to Paul.[9] In the letter to Philemon, Paul describes Timothy as "our brother" or "the brother," while elsewhere he speaks of him as a fellow slave, a coworker, and a "loved and trusted child in the Lord."[10] That last descriptor suggests that the relationship of Timothy to Paul is much like Paul's was to Barnabas, an impressive young protégé. Here, then, we see that Paul and Timothy write to Philemon.

Actually, to be more accurate, Paul writes "To Philemon our dearly loved coworker, Apphia our sister, Archippus our fellow soldier, and the church that meets in your house."[11] Let us note a few things about these recipients. Apphia might well have been Philemon's wife, and Archippus an adult son or another member of the household, given that Paul mentions the church in "your" (plural) house. Certainly they are, with Philemon, dear to Paul, as his language in describing them is quite affectionate. And "fellow soldier" suggests a high level of respect that Paul has for Archippus, who elsewhere is urged to press on in some unnamed task.[12] Most important, this letter is also addressed to the entire house church, though the request Paul makes is a personal one to Philemon himself, as the apostle-now-prisoner begins to address a very delicate situation.

As he moves from the salutation to the thanksgiving portion of the letter, Paul immediately makes it clear that he is speaking directly to Philemon, as the majority of occurrences of "you" and "your" here and in the remainder of the letter are, in the original Greek, in the singular, not plural tense. "Philemon, I thank my God every time I mention you in my prayers because I've heard of your love and faithfulness, which you have both for the Lord Jesus and for all God's people."[13] And thus it continues on from there. Paul has heard of Philemon's good work, and expressly states that he has been greatly encouraged by that work, specifically that "the hearts of God's people are refreshed by your actions, my brother."[14] Paul will come back to this image momentarily, but for now moves on to the body of the missive and his request.

"[I] appeal to you for my child Onesimus. I became his father in the faith during my time in prison."[15] Now the penny drops! Up until now, Paul has been singing Philemon's praises, with his words presumably being read in the midst of the congregation that would meet in Philemon's home. Now, having heard of all that Philemon has done for the saints, that congregation bears witness as Paul asks Philemon to do one more thing for a specific member of the body of Christ, his runaway slave, Onesimus. Having met him in prison and seen the captured slave's passion and gifts, Paul not only shared the gospel with Onesimus but also nurtured him as an apprentice. Now the time has come for his spiritual child to be released, and so Paul writes this brief but pointed letter to the slave's former master. In a wonderful play on words with Onesimus's name, which in Greek means "useful," Paul admits that he previously had been "useless" to Philemon, but now through his conversion to Christ has finally begun to live into his name and could be "useful" to Paul and Philemon alike.[16]

Paul goes so far as to say that, whatever Onesimus's reasons for running away, the fact is that divine providence might have had a hand in all this, so that he might be reunited to Philemon forever, "no longer as a slave but more than a slave—that is, as a dearly loved brother."[17] Onesimus already has become dear to Paul himself, so much so that the apostle admits he would love to have the former slave stay with him, but he wants to do the right thing and not act behind Philemon's back. The apostle even promises to repay any debt incurred by Onesimus, although he also not-so-subtly reminds Philemon that Philemon owes Paul far more, for he first came to know Christ through Paul. In Christ, Paul is a father to them both, and in Christ, they are now brothers. So even as Onesimus has become dear to Paul, so the apostle hopes he might become dear to Philemon as well. In yet another play on words, Paul says he is sending Onesimus, who is "my own heart," back to Philemon. Only moments before, Paul had praised Philemon for the way in which he refreshed the hearts of God's people. Now he asks Philemon to "refresh my heart in Christ," his heart of course being Onesimus.[18] With final greetings from Epaphras, "who is in prison with me for the cause of Christ Jesus," as well as from (John) Mark, Aristarchus, Demas, and Luke, Paul wraps up this brief, but important epistle.[19]

The letter to Philemon is, then, an intensely personal plea about a particular situation. Its importance, however, lies in the fact that the circumstances Paul addresses were far from unique in first-century society and, thus, in first-century churches. As the church grew, as both slaves and masters came into the body of Christ, their social status and interrelationships became more and more complex. For this very reason, Paul's personal plea to Philemon could have served as a template for other relationships of dependence, if believers were truly ready to give priority to their life together in Christ.

Slaves and Slavery in Paul's Other Letters

Do note that the word itself, "slave," or *doulos* in Greek, only appears in a single verse in the letter to Philemon. But it may be found many times throughout other parts of the Pauline collection. The greatest preponderance of appearances is in Galatians and Romans, each having over a dozen verses where we find some variation of the word. It is also found to a lesser extent in

2 Corinthians and Philippians, as well as Ephesians, Colossians, 1 Timothy, and Titus. What is interesting is the different ways the word is used in the disputed versus undisputed letters.[20] In the disputed letters, there are more examples of the word *slave* being used literally to speak of an actual slave or slaves, while in the undisputed letters the word is overwhelmingly used in a more figurative sense. Allow me to explain.

Consider the following from the disputed letters.[21] From Colossians: "Slaves, obey your masters on earth in everything. Don't just obey like people pleasers when they are watching. Instead, obey with the single motivation of fearing the Lord." From Ephesians: "As for slaves, obey your human masters with fear and trembling and with sincere devotion to Christ. Don't work to make yourself look good and try to flatter people, but act like slaves of Christ carrying out God's will from the heart." From 1 Timothy: "Those who are under the bondage of slavery should consider their own masters as worthy of full respect so that God's name and our teaching won't get a bad reputation. And those who have masters who are believers shouldn't look down on them because they are brothers. Instead, they should serve them more faithfully, because the people who benefit from your good service are believers who are loved." And, finally, from Titus: "Tell slaves to submit to their own masters and please them in everything they do. They shouldn't talk back or steal. Instead, they should show that they are completely reliable in everything so that they might make the teaching about God our savior attractive in every way."

These four passages share some things in common. First, as mentioned, these passages concern actual slaves; there is no metaphor or analogy here. These are real human beings who truly and literally are enslaved, owned as property by other human beings. Second, these passages are prescriptive, not descriptive. They are admonitions, instructions directed to the slaves, whether in direct "you" statements or indirectly as in "tell slaves to be . . ." Third, these passages all call for submission and obedience from the slaves, and not begrudgingly or just when they are being watched, but willingly and even wholeheartedly. These are fairly extraordinary statements, and strong reasons for people to accuse Paul of being pro-slavery and supporting the status quo of power differentials.

But, of course, the other, obvious thing these four passages have in common is that they are all from the disputed letters, the first two taken from the household codes of Colossians and Ephesians. We have already discussed the codes in which wives, children, and slaves—those without power in first-century Roman society—are advised to look with deference to those in power. Last chapter we saw that these particular letters, along with 2 Thessalonians and the Pastoral Letters, are considered by many scholars to have been written by someone other than Paul, using his name pseudonymously in order to give added weight to the writing. "If Paul was alive now, this is what he would say." The problem is that by putting words in Paul's mouth, it might be that they were actually having him say the *opposite* of what the apostle himself said in the undisputed letters. After all, the very purpose of these household codes in ancient times was to promote social stability, to preserve the status quo for the sake of harmony. At one time, Saul of Tarsus had been quite concerned about preserving the status quo, at least for the people of Israel, but Paul the apostle was concerned about something different: a new creation.

So, when we go back to one of Paul's earliest undisputed letters, Galatians, we find the familiar passage already mentioned here several times: "There is neither Jew nor Greek; there is neither slave nor free; nor is there male and female, for you are all one in Christ Jesus."[22] Almost immediately thereafter, in chapter 4 of Galatians, Paul goes on to contrast those who are what he calls the true children of Abraham, the father of faith, with those who are slaves and not heirs. These are the Christians who demand circumcision for converts to Christ. To Paul, they might spiritually descend from Abraham, but through Hagar, the "slave woman." Those who believe, who trust that they do not need to be circumcised in order to belong to God in Christ, are the spiritual descendants of Sarah, the "free woman." Here, we do not hear Paul calling on slaves to obey their masters, but rather we find him using the slave imagery in a negative light, allegorically contrasted with the freedom we find in Christ, not circumcision. "Therefore, brothers and sisters, we aren't the slave woman's children, but we are the free woman's children."[23] But just in case the believers in Galatia become selfish, he reminds them in chapter 5 to "don't let this freedom be an opportunity to indulge your selfish impulses,

118

but serve each other through love."[24] This is all about life in the household of God, not a typical Roman household.

Paul's correspondence with the Corinthian Christians again has nothing to say about actual slaves obeying their masters, but does speak of literal slaves, reminding those believers who were slaves when they were "called in the Lord"[25] are free in Christ and those who were free persons when called are now slaves of Christ. He urges them to "Don't become slaves of people,"[26] but points to himself as an example of one who has chosen to be a "slave to all people, to recruit more of them"[27] to Christ. In 2 Corinthians, he again describes his colleagues and himself as "your slaves for Jesus' sake."[28]

By the time we come to Romans and Philippians, letters written while in prison, we find another figurative use of slavery. Several times in the sixth chapter of his letter to the Romans, Paul contrasts those who are "slaves of sin" with those who by God's grace have become "slaves of righteousness."[29] He sounds almost embarrassed about his analogy, as he admits to "speaking with ordinary metaphors because of your limitations."[30] Later in the letter, he goes further to say that the "spirit of slavery"[31] is linked with what he sees as a false pride based on an obsessive adherence to the Jewish law, again contrasted with a "spirit of adoption" for those who recognize that by grace they have become children of God and heirs of salvation. In Philippians, Paul goes so far as to describe himself and Timothy as *douloi*, slaves or servants of Christ Jesus. Even more, he argues that the believers' call to serve one another in humility is grounded in Jesus's own "emptying" of himself, "taking the form of a slave" and giving his life on the cross.[32]

What a difference, then, in the use of slave terminology in the disputed and undisputed letters! A reading of the letters to the Galatians, Corinthians, Romans, and Philippians reveals a consistency in using slavery in more figurative or allegorical ways, always with an eye toward lifting up our status as beloved children of God as contrasted with slaves of sin, of the law, of earthly ways. And when it is used in a prescriptive sense, then it is usually not towards literal slaves who need to obey their masters, but toward fellow Christians who should willingly serve one another as slaves for Jesus's sake. Unlike those passages likely written by others later, in which "Paul" appears far more concerned about stability in a household, in the undisputed letters, there is a consistent focus instead on the only household that truly concerned Paul: the household of God.

Turning the World Upside Down

Of course, the irony in all of this is that just as Paul was not trying to support the societal status quo, neither was he trying to be a social reformer. As noted, his focus was almost entirely on a single group of people within society, what he called the "church." Now we are so used to this term that we may not realize what a fascinating choice of words Paul created to describe this new thing that he, with Barnabas, helped birth. The Greek word that is translated "church" is *ekklēsia*, and in Paul's time it referred generally to a gathered assembly and more specifically to the assembly of free landowning citizens of a city, in other words, those who enjoyed the privileges of citizenship and were therefore peers of one another. Even in the Greek translation of the Hebrew scriptures, the Septuagint, *ekklēsia* was used to speak of the assembly of Israelites, peers, and kinsmen gathered together to hear the Mosaic Law.[33] Thus, Paul chooses a word with significant secular and political meaning, implying that those "in Christ" can expect the kind of rights, equality, and usefulness that a city's citizens would enjoy in the secular *ekklēsia*.

Herein lies the paradox of Paul. In one sense, he appears to be quite sectarian, concerned solely with this countercultural community called the church, and not at all with the outside world.[34] Yet what happens in the church in no way stays in the church, as Paul's evangelistic efforts ensure a constant expansion of the church's boundaries, welcoming all types and conditions of individuals. They enter as Jews and Greeks. They come in as slaves and free. They enter as male and female. But Paul is clear that membership in this relational group trumps all other designations. To be "in Christ," then, means that the old designations disappear. It truly is a rebirth, and the relationships of members as sisters and brothers take priority over the old ones such as master and slave.

So by being "sectarian," by focusing on the internal relationships and roles of the Christian *ekklēsia*, Paul actually subverts the outside social system as well. For how can Philemon welcome back Onesimus as a slave (in the outside world) once he acknowledges him as a newly adopted brother (in the Christian *ekklēsia*)? The result of their internal life together cannot help but affect their external roles and relationship as well. This goes far beyond what was happening in Jerusalem with the Jewish sectarian movement known as "the Way." By intentionally making room in the church for all people, and then by helping them see that their identity within takes priority over outside classifications, the stage is set for overall transformation. What a remarkable thing! Paul goes from city to city, creates these house churches in which members are all brothers and sisters of one another, and then watches as their spiritual DNA is transformed and replicates itself. Is Paul a social reformer? No, he is something far more radical. Paul is the spiritual midwife for a new creation, upending all the old ways of defining and categorizing people.

Indeed, the phrase from Acts used of Paul and his companions, saying that they "have been disturbing the peace throughout the empire," or (in the NRSV translation) "turned the world upside down," is not empty hyperbole.[35] By empowering women as fellow workers and by arguing for the liberation of a runaway slave, Paul helps shift the ways in which these first Christians understand themselves not only in relationship to God but also in relation to one another and to the world. Of course, this means resistance and reaction. It is one thing to open the doorway to Gentile converts, for this only upsets the delicate balance of one small ethnic and religious subset of the vast empire. But empowering women and slaves is a more serious thing, much more threatening to the status quo of existing relationships grounded in notions of superiority and inferiority, power and dependence.

But what of a passage from Romans (one of the undisputed letters) where, although his words here are not directed specifically to slaves, the apostle directs that "every person should place themselves under the authority of the government" and even goes so far as to say that "the authorities that are there have been put in place by God."[36] Much debate has been sparked through the ages about this passage, and how it seems to be the ultimate caving in to the societal status quo. But look at what immediately follows the passage about submission to authority: "pay everyone what you owe them. Pay the taxes you owe, pay the duties you are charged, give respect to those you should respect, and honor those you should honor."[37] If this sounds familiar, it should. We hear an echo of Jesus's words to those who questioned him about paying taxes to the pagan Caesar. Jesus asked whose likeness was on the coins that every-. one carried. When told it was that of the emperor, he offered a retort that is well known to this day: "Give to Caesar what belongs to Caesar and to God what belongs to God."[38] With these words, Jesus and Paul both suggest that it might not be wise to go up against societal powers head-on, for as Paul states the obvious, the secular authorities wield the sword—and God allows it. Here again we find an echo of Jesus when standing before the Roman procurator, Pilate: "You would have no authority over me if it had not been given to you from above."[39] No confrontation but no fear either.

Now there are some who have used Paul's call for submission to authority to argue that Paul advocated stability and the preservation of the status quo. But what if he is instead following in his former mentor's footsteps? Ah, we finally return to Barnabas! We should never forget that while Stephen the Martyr went head to head with religious reactionaries and lost his life as a result, Barnabas the Encourager instead quietly used relational bridge-building and intentional mentoring to bring about lasting change. In a similar manner, Paul speaks of respecting the outside authority, but simultaneously offers a way of transforming relationships so as to disarm that power and authority. And in his letter to Philemon he does all this with a smile and a word of appreciation to the one who has refreshed the hearts of God's people. So while on the one hand Paul appears indifferent to the outside world, concerning himself almost completely with life inside the *ekklēsia* of God, on the other hand the transformed relationships of those within that assembly influence their outside relationships as well, thereby contributing, intentionally or otherwise, to the transformation of society, one soul at a time.

Dangerous People

So, as with women, how did Paul, the advocate for freedom, become the preserver of power? How did the one who encourages a runaway slave become the one who confronts slaves and tells them to obey their masters with all their heart? To answer this, it might be helpful to move forward several centuries to consider another well-known hero of the faith, Giovanni Bernardone, better known to us as Francis of Assisi. People think they know Francis—the animal lover, the bird lover, Mother Nature's son—but, in truth, to the powers that be, he was a dangerous man. Part of the reason was his message of poverty and simplicity. In a medieval age where the walls between the haves and the have-nots were seemingly impenetrable, Francis broke down the walls and repaired the breaches. "Rebuild my church," he once heard the Almighty say to him, and he set out to do that. He literally transformed ruins into renewed places of worship, even as he helped shape the lives of thousands who joined in his mad crusade of simplicity.

Through the orders he formed, people began to notice changes. As those in power nervously looked on, not just those on the fringe of society but the best and the brightest renounced their inheritances and joined the Friars Minor (for men) or the Poor Clares (for women). Particularly subversive was what Francis called the "Brotherhood of Repentance," that Third Order that welcomed people who were not prepared to become friars or nuns but desired a rule of life and a way of living into the gospel. Those who previously had defined themselves and others around them by societal standards of wealth and power now willingly looked at life through radically different lenses. Add to this the willingness of the poor man from Assisi to cross enemy lines during the height of the Crusades and to meet with the Islamic sultan to talk about faith and spirituality, and it becomes easy to see why Francis was a threat to the status quo, much like Paul before him. Like Paul's challengers, the only way that those in power could effectively combat the threat Francis posed was to lift him up as a saint even as they edited him by creating a new Rule for the Franciscans that was less countercultural and more palatable for those who wanted order, not transformation. And so the man who single-handedly challenged the socioeconomic realities of medieval Europe by creating a movement of transformed lives and relationships soon became known as the eccentric but loveable proto hippie.

Paul recognized from the start the dangers posed by the Jesus movement. He saw what Peter and the other apostles seemed to miss: that by empowering individual lives, Christ transforms relationships and systems. The barriers between Jews and Gentiles would necessarily break down. Likewise, if all are sisters and brothers in the Christian *ekklēsia*, then they can hardly go back to defining themselves as inferiors and superiors in the rest of life. If taken seriously, equality in the church results in emancipation in life. Returning to Acts, there is a wonderful story of a slave girl possessed by a spirit of divination who follows Paul and his colleagues and cries out about them, "These people are servants of the Most High God! They are proclaiming a way of salvation to you!"[40] After days of this, an annoyed Paul drives out the demon from her, and she is made free. The slave of God liberates an enslaved young woman. And, not surprisingly, the slave owners immediately throw Paul and his companions in prison for disturbing the peace, rocking the boat, turning things upside down. Of course, Paul escapes. But a different, and much more effective way of dealing with this troublemaker, has come through household codes and pseudonymous epistles, as the apostle has become shackled to a reputation as a misogynist and supporter of slavery. And like Francis, it has been far more difficult for the Paul—the prisoner who wrote so eloquently to Philemon on behalf of a runaway slave—to escape from those bonds.

Human Like You

A final word should be added, and it comes again from Acts. You will recall that before their split, before even the climatic events of the Jerusalem Council, the apostolic duo faced a crowd who saw the power that emanated from them and lifted them up as deities. In one of those moments when the Encourager is named first, we are told that Barnabas and Paul tore their clothing and cried out to the crowd, "People, what are you doing? We are humans too, just like you! We are proclaiming the good news to you."[41] Paul had learned from personal experience that Jesus changes everything. When the apostles were afraid of him because of what he had done and been in his previous life, Barnabas vouched for him and took him as an apprentice. The Encourager showed how Jesus makes all things new.

Even so, the two together try to explain to a crowd that they are "human like you." The love of God in Christ is the great equalizer, so that we don't have to make ourselves greater by seeing others as lesser. Slavery makes no sense in the household of God, where all are sisters and brothers in Christ. Power differentials break down in the body of Christ, where every member is interdependent on the others, where none are to be dismissed as weaker or less honorable. And any person who was only viewed as useless, when viewed through the lenses of the Spirit, when seen as a new creation, is inherently worthy and incredibly useful. This is the legacy that Paul, following in Barnabas's footsteps, has left to the church. It is a travesty that others who sought to retain power remade the Liberator in their own likeness, and it is an even greater travesty that so many of us since have accepted that.

So what about us? Are our congregations really spiritual *ekklēsia*, where all are welcome and all are worthy? Are they truly households of God, where are all equal and all are valued? In the 1979 Episcopal *Book of Common Prayer*, the baptismal covenant is lifted up as the foundational statement about our Christian life. If we say we believe in God who created us, in Christ who redeemed us, in the Spirit who walks with us and empowers us, then we necessarily will strive, with God's help, to live into the other promises we make: to meet regularly for worship and fellowship and learning; to acknowledge our failings and turn our lives around; to respect the dignity of every human being; to love as Christ has loved us. If we take these promises seriously, then our congregations will be places where heaven and earth meet. If we take these promises seriously, then our congregations can be the first wave of the transformation of the world. After all, isn't that what Paul the apostle, the prisoner, the liberator said all along?

Discussion Questions

1. Was this your first time reading Philemon? If so, what were your first impressions of the letter? If you have read it before, what did you remember about it?

2. Roman society placed great importance on the loyalty and obligation due to a patron—do we have an equivalent to "patrons" today? What would you say are the obligations expected of you? How easy is it to balance them?

3. Paul was quite creative in how he described the Christian community. In twenty-five words or fewer, how would you describe your own parish community in an advertisement to potential new members *without* using any specifically religious terms?

4. What are some things your congregation could do internally that ultimately would be influential and possibly transformative in the surrounding community?

5. What is your reaction to hearing about the influence Francis of Assisi had on the socioeconomic system of his time? Are there others in our own time who have posed a threat to the status quo, and how do our systems of power deal with them?

Conclusion
Moving beyond Stereotypes

A sarcophagus dating to around the year 390 CE, with remains inside carbon-dated to the first century, was unearthed in 2006 in the Basilica of St. Paul's Outside-the-Walls, Rome. A simple inscription on the tomb reads *Paulo Apostolo Mart.*—"Paul, Apostle, Martyr." Tradition has long held that Paul was executed sometime around 64 or 65 CE, outside the imperial capital where the basilica bearing his name now stands. Unlike Peter, who is said to have died by the agonizing means of crucifixion, Paul was a Roman citizen by birth, and therefore was afforded a more "humane" execution by beheading. Over twelve hundred miles to the east, in Salamis on the isle of Cyprus, according to tradition, a jealous mob, upon seeing the success that followed Barnabas in his preaching ministry, stoned him to death, much like that other Hellenist, Stephen, years before. Barnabas and Paul had long since gone their separate ways, and they faced death in different places. But these remarkable figures are forever linked through Luke's account in Acts.

That account, interestingly, does not show us Paul's demise, much less that of Barnabas. Instead, at the close of Acts we find Paul in Rome preaching, teaching, reaching out to all who will listen and respond. In truth, the story of Acts does not end at all. The curtain does not fall. What happens is that the mission so ably taken on by Barnabas and Paul is now our mission. We are their heirs. It is all the more important, therefore, that we move beyond the stereotypes that have grown up through the years—around Paul in particular—and, as mentioned from the start, dare to let go of some of our old and perhaps strongly held assumptions.

Before talking about those assumptions, let's take one more look at some of the players we have encountered on this stage. Almost all of them have been good people, even heroic (let's forget Ananias and Sapphira, shall we?). Yet they all approached Jesus's Great Commission in vastly different ways.

For Peter and the rest of the Twelve, the commission meant perpetuating a both/and situation in which faithful Jews who came to believe in Jesus as the Messiah could join the apostles in a communal existence—praying and reading their beloved scriptures through new lenses—while remaining tied to the daily temple routine. Using Jesus's own metaphor, we might say that they placed the new wine of the gospel in the old wineskins of familiar traditions. As the Way, they experienced tremendous initial growth, but by remaining a temple-based Jewish sect, they reached a glass ceiling. New, nonlocal members wanted the "wine" they offered but had little use for the "wineskin" that seemed to come with it.

One such person was Stephen who, as one of the Seven, is another player to have briefly crossed our stage. For Stephen, a Hellenist Jew, Jesus made the temple and all that it represented irrelevant. We have only one recorded sermon attributed to him in Acts, and yet it was offensive enough to certain religious traditionalists that they stoned him for it.

Stephen's killers were outsiders, not in any way a part of the Way, but there were other Jews equally zealous for the traditional ways who did come to embrace the gospel. They seemed to respect Peter and the other leaders in Jerusalem, but resisted any notion that there could be membership in the Jesus movement without first being circumcised as a prerequisite for entry. These Judaizers, as Paul would call them, firmly believed that anything less was completely unacceptable.

Although James, the brother of Jesus, arrived onstage rather late in the story, he immediately took on a leading role, having at some point become recognized as the de facto leader of the Jerusalem community. His primary goal was unity, and he did his utmost to keep everyone happy and remaining at the table, though his preferences appeared to be towards the traditionalists. For James, a both/and situation was possible if the more extreme group would simply maintain a low profile and avoid doing anything that would obviously set off their more conservative fellow believers.

128

And then, of course, there are our two chief protagonists, Barnabas and Paul. More than anything else, they were change agents, opening wide the door to Gentiles without requiring circumcision in order to belong. Antioch was their base and their training ground. While honoring many of the traditions inherited from the Jerusalem believers and intentionally retaining ties with them, these new apostles immersed themselves in a more pragmatic and inclusive kind of community in Antioch. There, a new creation—Christians—blossomed and flourished and soon replicated itself in urban centers throughout the empire. Barnabas and Paul's success resulted in resistance, not only before, but also after, the supposedly conflict-ending edict of the Jerusalem Council. And while Barnabas and Paul together seemed to be able to weather any storm that came from outside, as soon as resistance came from the recognized leaders like Peter or James, Barnabas seemed to falter, and the great partnership was undone.

At its heart, despite the equal billing on the marquee, our tale has ultimately been about Paul and those assumptions propagated about him through the centuries, preventing countless Christians from truly hearing what he had to say. Paul was indeed confrontational, but what he confronted was a status quo that pushed some down and out. In this sense, we can begin to appreciate the fact that, in the end, Paul inherited not only the leadership role from Barnabas but also the role of encourager. Just as he himself was once welcomed and trained by Barnabas—despite serious misgivings on the part of the Jerusalem leaders—so Paul, with Barnabas, did the same for uncircumcised believers. And supposedly the recognized leaders affirmed their work. But, as we have seen, this was not really, truly the case. And Peter, John Mark and, yes, "even Barnabas," caved in the face of pressure and left the Gentiles feeling like outsiders all over again. So Paul's confrontations—with Cephas/Peter, with John Mark, and with his longtime partner—were actually the ultimate sign of encouragement to the many powerless ones who thought that the church meant what it said about grace and belonging in Christ. Paul was willing to confront the powers-that-be, and thus risk incurring accusations of being a troublemaker, because he believed in every fiber of his being that in Christ we, individually and together, become a new creation; the old is gone, the new has come. And, as we have also seen in both Acts and even more in his own undisputed letters, Paul believed this was true not only in terms of ethnicity but also in terms of gender and socioeconomic status. In Christ, there is neither . . .

How, then, did Paul gain a reputation so very different from what Acts and his own writings seem to say about him? How did the leader who opposed Barnabas precisely because the latter did *not* stand up for those in need become known instead as the reactionary who held back the revolutionary power of the Christian gospel? We have considered this, but it is important to reiterate here at the end that whenever the church has been unable to condemn or remove a leader who upsets the equilibrium, it often moves to canonize the individual while somehow also "editing" his or her reputation.

In the Russian classic *The Brothers Karamazov*, Fyodor Dostoyevsky presents a story-within-a-story entitled "The Grand Inquisitor," in which Jesus returns to earth during the time of the Inquisition, when the church was at its zenith of power, only to be arrested and imprisoned for causing trouble.[1] The Grand Inquisitor himself comes to visit Jesus and carefully explains that the latter could not possibly be allowed to roam free and speak to the masses about their free will. After all, the Inquisitor tells him, the church had worked for years to set up an effective system of control and societal harmony, and it could not afford to have its Founder mess it all up. The result could be chaos, anarchy, unhappiness. No, the Inquisitor concluded, for the sake of the people Jesus had to be locked up. It was fine for him to be worshipped, but unacceptable for him to be emulated. Is it any wonder that decades later, in America, the Roman Catholic social activist Dorothy Day once said, "Don't call me a saint; I don't want to be dismissed that easily."[2]

The church has always lived in the tension of being both a part of, and apart from, the surrounding culture. That culture, whether social or ecclesiastical, has often injected the body of Christ with its own preexisting sets of prejudices and power plays. In the first-century Roman Empire, this meant that certain people were on top while others were not. What Paul and Barnabas did in Antioch and beyond was nothing short of remarkable, for they helped initiate a truly countercultural alternative system in which all such assumptions were thrown out. It is therefore no surprise that those in power, those who like Dostoyevsky's Grand Inquisitor sought to maintain control, would find Barnabas and Paul's experiment to be unacceptable. After their split, with his martyrdom and the wide circulation of his letters, Paul became an even more dangerous person. The only way to disarm him was essentially to put words in the apostle's mouth.

In his classic work *What's Wrong with the World*, the noted British novelist and essayist G. K. Chesterton said, "The Christian ideal has not been tried and found wanting; it has been found difficult and left untried."[3] Well, Barnabas and Paul tried, and unsurprisingly they met resistance, first from without and then from within. Barnabas modeled for his protégé what it meant to be an encourager, but then buckled under pressure. The issue of their break was not because Barnabas put people before the task, and Paul cold-heartedly did not. It was not simply about giving someone a second chance, which Paul above all would appreciate. No, at the heart of their split was the failure to stand up for those who needed them. The Encourager stepped back from the very ideal that he first shared with Paul, an ideal that proved too difficult for Peter, for John Mark, for Barnabas himself. For Paul, however, the ideal was always about people, and they were worth it!

Now it is our time on the stage. It is our time to encourage those who come to us with hope in their hearts and gifts to share. It is our time to confront those who seek control and comfort over hospitality and unity. On a personal note, I teach a seminary course entitled "The Barnabas Principle" that sets out an innovative, holistic approach to congregational development and church leadership that I believe is desperately needed in our twenty-first-century context. The course focuses on areas such as goal setting, structural analysis, newcomer recruitment and retention, community outreach, visionary budgeting, and financial stewardship—all using Barnabas from Acts as the biblical model.[4] Throughout the course, I point to the many ways in which our congregations fall short of Jesus's Commission, usually because we are afraid of the unfamiliar. My students and I swap stories about parishes that, far from exuding a spirit of welcome and encouragement, instead make it clear that they exist primarily for the sake of the insiders.

I call the course "The Barnabas Principle" because I do believe that this little-known character exemplified the Christian ideal when he intentionally chose to stand by Paul and together build communities of belonging and mutual encouragement in Christ. If I was being completely honest, I would call it "The Paul Principle," as it is Barnabas's one-time apprentice who truly lived out the ideal and fought to make it a reality. But the sad truth is that people might not be attracted to a course called "The Paul Principle" precisely because of the effective spin job that was done on the apostle. As said already in these pages, I shake my head in amazement every time I hear Christians speak in glowing terms of Peter while remaining critical of Paul, even though it was "the chief of the apostles" who failed to stand up for the Gentiles in Antioch when it was inconvenient to do so, and it was Paul who dared to stand up to the beloved leader on their behalf. But because many Christians still hold onto the stereotypes, I look to Barnabas to provide the bridge to a more accurate, and far more powerful, view of Paul.

So, what will we do? Will we welcome, truly welcome outsiders and help them find their place in the household of God? Will we further assist in the development of their gifts and calling so that they in turn can be agents of transformation? Will we empower and encourage for the love of Christ, and risk the possibility of change for our own familiar, comfortable systems? These are difficult tasks that are required of us, but if we each would dare to be a Barnabas, if we would together follow in the footsteps of Paul, then we will boldly echo the words of our baptismal promises and proclaim in both word and deed, "I will, with God's help." And in those moments, if we listen carefully, we might just hear the sound not of quarreling, but of laughter and song, as Barnabas and Paul, once separated, are reunited through us once more.

Appendix
The Barnabas Principle

<u>B</u>egin with the big picture.

- What was essential to our congregation when it was founded?

- How has that understanding of identity and purpose changed in the years since then?

- How would we define the church's identity and purpose, its "sacred bundle" now?

<u>A</u>rrange structures strategically.

- Do all our structures line up with our defining principles and vision, our sacred bundle?

- How do we define our roles as vestry members/leaders in our church?

- What does our budget say about our priorities?

<u>R</u>etain and recruit newcomers.

- Take a field trip of your communications system, your property, and your services

- Be ambassadors and not simply greeters

- Create an ongoing record of your inclusion of newcomers, and pray for them

<u>N</u>urture future leaders.

- Think of those whom you would like to mentor

- Consider how you can share what you have learned from your time in leadership

- Make exit interviews standard procedure for volunteers and staff

Ask for direction and support.

- Seek the feedback and ideas of the Council of the Wise

- Grade yourselves on key areas of ministry through an every member canvas

- Pray!

Become a church for the community.

- Move beyond the standard ideas of outreach and ask what your community needs

- Form a task force to learn more about the demographics of your area

- Plan two or three "intersection" projects over an eighteen-month period and publicize

Analyze membership and giving patterns.

- Explore trends in people's attendance and involvement over several years

- Examine giving patterns in terms of different demographic categories like age/generation

- Consider how to educate newer members about your budget, so they are in the know

Specify a strategic pledging plan.

- Break predictable timing patterns, and move towards a year-round stewardship plan

- Create a Vestry stewardship statement, signed "unanimously and enthusiastically"

- Personalize the pledge program

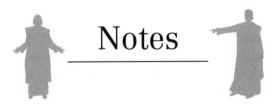

Notes

A Word about Acts

1. "Proper 28," in "Collects: Contemporary," in *The Book of Common Prayer* (New York: Church Publishing, 2011), 236.

Introduction

1. 1 Cor 14:34.

2. Col 3:22.

3. Luke 8:2-3. See also Mark 19:9-11, a later passage not contained in the earliest texts of Mark's Gospel, which reiterates Luke's description.

4. For more about Magdalene, see my book *A Dangerous Dozen: 12 Christians Who Threatened the Status Quo but Taught Us to Live Like Jesus* (Woodstock, VT: SkyLight Paths, 2011), 19–30.

5. This book follows the widely accepted tradition that Acts is the second of a two-volume work that is attributed to Luke, Paul's traveling companion commonly known as "the dearly loved physician" (Col 4:14). For more on Lukan authorship, see James D. G. Dunn, *Acts of the Apostles*, Epworth Commentaries (London: Epworth, 1997), Luke Timothy Johnson, *The Acts of the Apostles*, Sacra Pagina Series 5 (Collegeville, MN: Liturgical Press, 1992), and William H. Willimon, *Acts*, Interpretation (Louisville: John Knox Press, 1988).

6. Acts 2:44.

7. Acts 4:32, 34.

8. See David Wenham, *Paul: Follower of Jesus or Founder of Christianity?* (Grand Rapids: Eerdmans, 1995).

9. See my book *Transforming Stewardship* (New York: Church Publishing, 2009), xx.

135

10. Martin Luther King Jr., "Remaining Awake Through a Great Revolution" (sermon, National Cathedral, Washington, DC, on March 31, 1968).

11. See Luke 4:18-19. The passage Jesus reads is from Isa 61, and was considered by many Jews to be a passage pointing to the Messiah, the promised one sent by God to save God's chosen people.

12. Luke 4:24-27.

13. Luke 2:32.

14. In the Lukan account, Jesus's appointment of apostles follows a night spent in prayer (6:12), a point not found in the other Synoptics. Other significant moments in Luke's Gospel that occur either as Jesus is praying or immediately thereafter include the transfiguration (9:29), the teaching of the Lord's Prayer (11:1), and even the beginning of the passion (22:45). A similar pattern is reflected in the book of Acts (1:14; 10:31; 12:5). It is little wonder that the Lukan Jesus urges his disciples "to pray continuously" (18:1).

15. Luke 9:1-2.

16. Luke 8:1.

17. Luke 6:17 and 8:1; see also Mark 4:10. This view is echoed later in the Apostolic Father Clement's *On Virginity II*, 15.1: "Our Lord Himself was constantly with His twelve disciples when He had come forth to the world."

18. Cf. J. D. Kingsbury, *Conflict in Luke: Jesus, Authorities, Disciples* (Minneapolis: Fortress, 1991): "Sent to proclaim the kingdom of God and to heal, Jesus sends the Twelve to proclaim . . . and to heal" (p. 115).

19. Matt 10:5.

20. Luke 9:3-5; cf. Mark 6:8-11.

21. Matt 10:17-18

22. Luke 9:45, contrasted with Matt 13:51; 16:12; 17:13.

23. Mark 9:40-41.

24. Luke 9:53.

25. Interestingly, while Jesus's instructions to the Twelve in Luke 9 are quite brief, the comments to the Seventy constitute a much longer section, corresponding with the commissioning of the Twelve in Matt 10.

26. Cf. Luke 10:18 contrasted with 9:10.

27. Matt 10:6.

28. Num 11:16, 24-25.

29. Num 11:26-30.

30. Cf. Fred Craddock, *Luke* (*Interpretation*; Louisville: John Knox Press, 1990), 144–45.

31. Luke 10:2.

32. Luke 9:49.

1. Dangerous Newcomers

1. Acts 1:6.

2. It is interesting to note that no mention is made of the Spirit's involvement in the decision-making process for a twelfth apostle. Whatever the case, while so much attention is given to the selection of a twelfth apostle, after this Matthias never appears again in Luke's narrative.

3. Acts 1:6-8.

4. Matt 28:18-20.

5. Matt 28:19.

6. Acts 1:8.

7. Lewis's phrase is actually "further up and further in" and is found throughout *The Last Battle*, the final installment in his Chronicles of Narnia series.

8. As Lev 23:15-16 explains: "You must count off seven weeks starting with the day after the Sabbath, the day you bring the bundle for the uplifted offering; these must be complete. You will count off fifty days until the day after the seventh Sabbath. Then you must present a new grain offering to the LORD."

9. Acts 2:7.

10. Acts 2:14-36; 3:12-26; 4:8-12; 5:29-32. Theirs is a basic message, a "kerygma" linking the promises of the Hebrew prophets of old with the person and work of Jesus of Nazareth. For more about the specific nature and form of the apostolic kerygma, see my book *The Kerygma of Billy Graham* (Minneapolis: Worldwide Press, 1987).

11. "Wonders and signs," to use Luke's language in Acts 2:43 and 5:12.

12. Acts 3:1-2.

13. Luke 24:49.

14. Acts 4:32-37.

15. Ps 41:1.

16. Prov 14:31.

17. Tabitha—Acts 9:36; Cornelius—10:2; Paul—24:17.

18. Acts 2:44-45.

19. Acts 4:32-35.

20. Deut 15:7.

21. Lev 25:35.

22. Justin Martyr, I *Apology* 14:2-3.

23. Aristotle, *Nicomachean Ethics* 8.9, cited in M. Eugene Boring, Klaus Berger, and Carsten Colpe, eds., *Hellenistic Commentary to the New Testament* (Nashville: Abingdon, 1995), 313.

24. Josephus, *War* 2.122, beginning after line 119.

25. See Boring, Berger, and Colpe, *Hellenistic Commentary*, 313n491.

26. Acts 4:37 NRSV.

27. John 12:3 and 13:5, respectively.

28. Gerasene demoniac—Luke 8:35; Mary, sister of Martha—10:39; Jairus—8:41; Samaritan leper—17:16.

29. Acts 10:35 and 22:3, respectively. "At the feet" is found in the NRSV and other translations.

30. Acts 7:58. "At the feet" is found in the NRSV and other translations.

31. This is an important point to remember while examining later in this chapter the grievances of the Greek-speaking widows in Acts 6.

32. Clement, *Stromata*, book 2, chapter 20, describes Barnabas as "one of the seventy and a co-worker of Paul."

33. Acts 4:32.

34. The legend is that the Septuagint is the result of the translating work of seventy Greek-proficient Hebrew scholars, hence the word form for seven, *septa*.

35. Acts 7:54-60.

36. Acts 6:1. The transition phrase "in those days" is employed often by Luke to signal a new phase in his narrative, indeed far more often than by other New Testament writers. See Luke 2:1 and 6:12, as well as Acts 1:15; 9:36; 11:27.

37. "Hellenists" (NRSV) or "Greek-speaking disciples" are mentioned twice more in Acts, in 9:28-29 and 11:19-20.

38. The church father John Chrysostom notes: "Observe, how even in the beginning the evils came not only from without, but also from within" and adds that "this was no small evil" (*Homily on Acts*, 14).

39. Acts 7:48.

40. Acts 9:4-5.

2. A Tale of Two Cities

1. Acts 2:14-36.

2. Acts 4:32.

3. It is important to distinguish this Antioch from fifteen other cities of the same name existing in the Empire, including Antioch of Pisidia, located in Asia Minor between the districts of Phrygua and Pisidia and mentioned in Acts 13.

4. Today the city is Antakya, in Turkey.

5. Acts 6:5.

6. See respectively Acts 9:32-35 compared with Luke 5:17-26 and Acts 9:36-43 as compared with Luke 8:40-42, 51-56.

7. Acts 10:15.

8. Acts 10:28-29.

9. Acts 11:18.

10. Jon 4:2.

11. Luke 7:1-10.

12. Acts 10:22.

13. Luke 2:32.

14. James D. G. Dunn, *The Acts of the Apostles* (Valley Forge, PA: Trinity Press, 1996), 153.

15. Acts 8:1, 4.

16. Acts 11:19-20.

17. Acts 11:24. Luke reserves such praise for a few in his two volumes, including Stephen, who is said to be "endowed by the Holy Spirit with exceptional faith" (Acts 6:5).

18. Acts 11:26.

19. See my book *Transforming Stewardship* (New York: Church Publishing, 2009).

3. A Brave New World

1. See Luke 3:1; 8:3; 13:31-32; 23:7-12; Acts 4:27.

2. Compare Acts 13:2 with Luke 6:12-16 and 9:1-2.

3. Acts 11:29-30.

4. Acts 13:9-10.

5. Acts 14:15.

6. Gal 1:1-2.

7. 1 Thess 1:1.

8. As a brief explanation, Paul's letters are arranged in the New Testament according to size, first to churches, beginning with the largest, Romans, and extending to 2 Thessalonians, and then to individuals, beginning with the largest, 1 Timothy, and extending to Philemon. But this is not the order in which they were actually written. Scholars have long dated in the following chronological order those letter recognized as undisputedly written by Paul: 1 Thessalonians, Galatians, 1 Corinthians, 2 Corinthians, Romans, Philippians, Philemon. Other letters bearing his name remain somewhat in question as to authorship, namely Ephesians, Colossians, and 2 Thessalonians. Still others, 1 and 2 Timothy and Titus, are thought by most scholars to have been written by others using Paul's name. I will speak more about this, and why it is important, in chapter 6.

9. Gal 1:13.

10. Gal 1:14.

11. Jer 1:5.

12. Gal 1:17.

13. 1 Cor 4:15.

14. 1 Cor 9:1-3.

15. 1 Cor 9:5.

16. 2 Cor 11:13.

17. 2 Cor 11:5; 12:11.

18. Rom 1:1.

19. Rom 15:22.

20. 1 Cor 15:8-10.

21. Rom 8:31.

22. 1 Cor 12:12. See also Eph 4:4.

23. 1 Cor 12:21.

24. 1 Cor 13:1.

25. 1 Cor 13:4-7.

4. To Honor or Accommodate

1. From the seventh Ode of the Roman poet Horace, cited in various places.

2. Acts 13:7.

3. Acts 13:9.

4. Acts 13:15.

5. Acts 13:16.

6. Acts 13:22.

7. Acts 13:38-39.

8. Acts 13:46.

9. Acts 14:12.

10. Ovid, *Metamorphoses* viii, in *Cambridge Latin Anthology* (New York: Cambridge University Press, 1996), 626–60.

11. Acts 14:17.

12. Acts 17:16.

13. Acts 17:23.

14. Acts 17:24-25.

15. Acts 17:28.

16. 1 Cor 14:16. The later verses in that chapter that pertain to women will be the focus of chapter 6.

17. Acts 15:2.

18. See Paul's comment in Gal 2:1 about how "after fourteen years I went up again to Jerusalem with Barnabas, taking Titus along with me," which may refer to this trip.

19. Acts 15:5.

20. Acts 15:1.

21. Acts 15:9. Consider Paul's words in Gal 3:28 that in Christ "there is neither Jew nor Greek."

22. Acts 15:10.

23. See, for instance, Mark 5:37 and Luke 8:51, where they are present for the raising of the daughter of Jairus; Mark 9:2, Matt 17:1, and Luke 9:28, where they witness the transfiguration of Jesus; and Mark 13:3, 14:33, and Matt 26:37, where they are with Jesus on the Mount of Olives and in Gethsemane. James is always mentioned before John, which might mean he was the older brother, and together they were nicknamed "sons of Thunder" (Mark 3:17). The two were rebuked by Jesus after suggesting that an unreceptive Samaritan village be destroyed by fire (Luke 9:54), and were told by him that one day they would drink the cup (of suffering) which he would drink (Mark 10:35-40; Matt 20:20-23).

24. See Mark 3:18; Matt 10:3; Luke 6:15; and Acts 1:13.

2

25. See Mark 15:40; Matt 27:56; and Luke 24:10. Some have suggested that he might be the same as the son of Alphaeus.

26. See Mark 6:3 and Matt 13:55. They are mentioned, though not named, in John 7:5.

27. The unnamed brothers are mentioned as being present on the occasion of the coming of the Spirit at Pentecost in Acts 2. James is named in 12:17, then in chapter 15, and again in 21:18. Paul mentions him by name in Gal 2:9 and 1 Cor 15:7.

28. Amos 9:11-12, but also see Zech 2:11 and Isa 45:21.

29. Acts 15:19.

30. In 1 Corinthians, for example, Paul goes so far as to say that he himself has no problem eating food offered to idols—a remarkable shift from his earlier days as a Pharisee—but he would abstain from such for the sake of a fellow Christian who still had a problem with it.

31. Paul addresses this problem as well in 1 Corinthians.

32. This and the following quotations come from 1 Cor 9–11. This particular verse is 9:20.

33. Acts 12:20.

34. Acts 15:21.

35. Acts 15:24.

36. 1 Cor 9:21-22.

5. To Include or Not to Include

1. Acts 15:36-41.

2. Acts 12:12.

3. 1 Pet 5:13. "The fellow-elect church in Babylon [a probable code word for Rome] greets you, and so does my son Mark."

4. Mark 14:51-52.

5. Col 4:10-11.

6. Gal 2:11-14.

7. The official name of the Washington National Cathedral is the Cathedral Church of Saint Peter and Saint Paul in the City and Diocese of Washington.

8. The epistle often called *1 Clement* (though the second letter to bear his name is a later, pseudonymous work) speaks of Peter's "numerous labors" culminating in his martyrdom, and then goes into greater detail in outlining Paul's sufferings and his

accomplishments, including having preached "both in the east and west . . . having taught righteousness to the whole world, and having come to the extreme limit of the west." This passage comes from chapter 5 of Clement's epistle.

9. In his other letters, the churches to which Paul writes are based in a city, like Corinth or Philippi. *Galatia* refers instead to a region, not a single city.

10. Gal 1:1.

11. Gal 1:6.

12. Gal 1:7, 9.

13. Gal 1:6.

14. Gal 2:2.

15. Gal 2:7.

16. Gal 2:12.

17. Gal 2:13.

18. Ibid.

19. Acts 17:6. The setting is Thessalonica.

20. 1 Thess 1:1.

21. 2 Cor 1:1; Phil 1:1; Phlm 1.

22. See Acts 19:29; 20:4; 27:2.

23. See Phlm 23–24 and Col 4:10-11, respectively.

24. 2 Cor 5:17.

25. Gal 3:28.

6. Neither Male nor Female

1. 1 Cor 14:34.

2. Ibid. NRSV.

3. Acts 1:14.

4. Acts 5:1-11.

5. Acts 9:36-42.

6. Acts 12:12-13.

7. Acts 16:13-14.

8. Acts 17:34.

9. Acts 18:2-3; also Acts 18:18; 18:26; 1 Cor 16:19; Rom 16:3; and 2 Tim 4:19.

10. The Roman writer Suetonius writes that the emperor "banished from Rome all the Jews, who were continually making disturbances at the instigation of one Chrestus" (*Claudius* 25).

11. Acts 24:24 and 25:13, 23, respectively.

12. Gal 3:28.

13. 2 Cor 5:17.

14. See Rom 16:1-16 for all that follows in this section.

15. Rom 16:13. The NRSV translation says, "Greet Rufus, who is chosen in the Lord; and greet his mother—a mother to me also."

16. 1 Cor 14:33-35.

17. 1 Cor 14:34-35.

18. 1 Cor 12:13.

19. Eph 5:22-24; Col 3:18; 1 Pet 3:1.

20. Aristotle, *Politics* 1.1253b.

21. Eph 6:5.

22. 1 Tim 2:11-12.

23. See Tertullian, *Of Baptism* 17.5.

24. For a concise overview of the impact of the Philadelphia Eleven on the Church's ties with the rest of the Anglican Communion and other ecumenical partners, see Mary Tanner, "The Conflict Over Women's Ordination: A Credible Model for Ecumenical Decision Making?" *Anglican and Episcopal History* 44 (1995): 429–43.

25. See resolution 1976-B300, "Express Mind of the House of Bishops on Irregularly Ordained Women," The Archives of the Episcopal Church, accessed August 29, 2014, http://www.episcopalarchives.org/cgi-bin/acts/acts_resolution-complete.pl?resolution=1976-B300. For more, see General Convention, *Journal of the General Convention of the Protestant Episcopal Church in the United States of America, otherwise known as The Episcopal Church, Minneapolis, 1976* (New York: General Convention, 1983), B–148.

26. *Works of Martin Luther* (Philadelphia Edition), trans. C.M. Jacobs, vol. 6: *Preface to the New Testament* (Grand Rapids: Baker Book House, 1982), 439–44.

27. From "Proper 28," in "Collects: Contemporary," in *The Book of Common Prayer* (New York: Church Publishing, 2011), 236.

28. The former quotation is found in Mark 9:40 and Luke 9:50, while the latter is found in Matt 12:30 and Luke 11:23.

29. Consider James D. G. Dunn, *The New Perspective on Paul* (Grand Rapids: Eerdmans, 2008).

30. Matt 22:34-39; also Mark 12:28-24, Here, Jesus merges the *Shema* of Deut 6:4-5 with the hospitality passage of Lev 19:33-34.

31. Madeline Albright, *Madam Secretary* (New York: Miramax Books, 2003), 663.

32. See "Resolutions from 1978: Resolution 21: Women in the Priesthood," The Lambeth Conference, accessed August 29, 2014, http://www.lambethconference .org/resolutions/1978/1978-21.cfm.

7. Useful to You and Me

1. Cited in my book *Conflict in Corinth: Redefining the System*, Studies in Biblical Literature, vol. 42 (New York: Peter Lang, 2001), 69.

2. From Philo's "Special Laws II" XXXIX (227), from Yongue, C. D., ed., *The Works of Philo*, 3rd ed. (Peabody, MA: Hendrickson, 1993), 589.

3. John 19:12.

4. Matt 6:24; Luke 16:13.

5. Phil 1:1. Other translations, such as the NRSV, say "servant."

6. Phil 2:8.

7. 2 Tim 1:5 speaks of Timothy being a third-generation Christian, as both his mother, Eunice, and his grandmother, Lois, were believers.

8. See 1 Thess 3:2-6; 1 Cor 16:10; Phil 2:19-23. Timothy is even mentioned in the anonymous letter to the Hebrews (13:23).

9. It should be remembered that the canonical collection of Paul's writings includes his undisputed letters (1 Thessalonians, Galatians, 1 Corinthians, 2 Corinthians, Romans Philippians, and Philemon), those letters whose authorship has been questioned by some scholars (2 Thessalonians, Ephesians, and Colossians), and the so-called Pastoral Letters (1 Timothy, 2 Timothy, Titus), which are regarded by most scholars as pseudonymous, written sometime after the apostle's death but attributed to him. As mentioned before, pseudonymous works were quite common in the ancient world, and there are numerous cases of them in post-New Testament writings (*Acts of Paul, Acts of Peter, Epistle of Barnabas, Gospel of Mary, Gospel of Thomas*, and so on).

10. See Phil 1:1 (slave); Rom 16:21 (coworker); 1 Cor 4:17 (loved and trusted).

11. Phlm 1-2.

12. Col 4:17: "See to it that you complete the ministry that you received in the Lord."

13. Phlm 4-5.

14. Phlm 7.

15. Phlm 10.

16. Phlm 11.

17. Phlm 16.

18. Phlm 20.

19. Phlm 23.

20. Please refer again to the previous chapter, where there is greater explanation of the "disputed" letters, namely Ephesians, Colossians, 2 Thessalonians, and the Pastoral Letters, all or some of which many scholars believe to have been written at a later time using Paul's name.

21. See respectively Col 3:22; Eph 6:5-6; 1 Tim 6:1-2; Titus 2:9-10.

22. Gal 3:28. It is repeated, but without the male/female pair, in 1 Cor 12:13.

23. Gal 4:31.

24. Gal 5:13.

25. 1 Cor 7:21.

26. 1 Cor 7:23.

27. 1 Cor 9:19.

28. 2 Cor 4:5.

29. Rom 6:15-23.

30. Rom 6:19.

31. Rom 8:15.

32. Phil 2:7.

33. See Deut 9:10; 18:16; 31:30, as well as Judg 20:2. Stephen's sermon in Acts 7:38 similarly uses *ekklēsia* to speak of the assembly of Israel in the wilderness.

34. Recommended here is a perennial classic by H. Richard Niebuhr, *Christ and Culture*, rev. ed. (New York: Harper, 2001), in which Niebuhr cites five categories of the church's relationship with the surrounding culture, all on a continuum ranging from separation from culture to agreement with culture. Although first published in 1951, the book still resonates and raises wonderful questions for us today.

35. Acts 17:6.

36. Rom 13:1.

37. Rom 13:7.

38. Mark 12:14-17.

39. John 19:11.

40. Acts 16:17.

41. Acts 14:14-15.

Conclusion

1. There are many editions of Dostoyevsky's classic *The Brothers Karamazov*. One such version is the Norton Critical Edition (second edition, 2011), translated and with a new introduction by Susan McReynolds Oddo.

2. See more in Dorothy Day, *Selected Writings*, ed. Robert Ellsberg (New York: Orbis, 2005).

3. A revised edition of this 1910 work, *What's Wrong with the World*, was published in 2009 by Seven Treasures Press.

4. For a brief overview of "The Barnabas Principle," see the appendix herein.

For Further Reading

Dixon, Suzanne. *The Roman Family*. Baltimore: Johns Hopkins University Press, 1992.

Dunn, James D. G. *Jesus, Paul, and the Gospels*. Grand Rapids: Eerdmans, 2011.

Ferlo, Roger. *Opening the Bible*. Vol. 2 of New Church's Teaching Series. Boston: Cowley, 1997.

Gaventa, Beverly Roberts. *Acts*. Abingdon New Testament Commentaries. Nashville: Abingdon, 2003.

Johnson, Luke. *Acts of the Apostles*. Sacra Pagina. Collegeville, MN: Liturgical, 1992.

Longenecker, Richard N. *The Road from Damascus: The Impact of Paul's Conversion on His Life, Thought, and Ministry*. Rev. ed. Grand Rapids: Eerdmans, 2002.

Meeks, Wayne A. *The First Urban Christians: The Social World of the Apostle Paul*. 2nd ed. New Haven, CT: Yale University Press, 2003.

Miller, Ron. *The Sacred Writings of Paul: Selections Annotated & Explained*. Woodstock, VT: SkyLight Paths, 2007.

Moots, Paul. *Becoming Barnabas: The Ministry of Encouragement*. Lanham, MD: Alban Books/Rowan & Littlefield, 2004.

Niebuhr, H. Richard. *Christ and Culture*. Rev. ed. New York: Harper, 2001.

Robertson, C. K. *A Dangerous Dozen: 12 Christians Who Threatened the Status Quo*. Woodstock, VT: SkyLight Paths, 2011.

———. *Conversations with Scripture: The Acts of the Apostles*. New York: Morehouse Publishing, 2010.

———. *Transforming Stewardship*. New York: Church Publishing, 2009.

Wade, Frank. *Transforming Scripture*. New York: Church Publishing, 2008.

Willimon, William H. *Acts*. Interpretation. Louisville: Westminster John Knox, 2010.

Zabriskie, Marek P. *The Bible Challenge: Read the Bible in a Year*. Cincinnati: Forward Movement, 2012.